STRAWBERRY PLAIN
AUDUBON CENTER

STRAWBERRY PLAINS AUDUBON CENTER

Four Centuries of a Mississippi Landscape

For cousin Allison —

Best,
Hubert

Hubert H. McAlexander

University Press of Mississippi

Jackson

Audubon®

www.upress.state.ms.us

The University Press of Mississippi is a member of the Association of American University Presses.

First printing 2008

∞

Library of Congress Cataloging-in-Publication Data

McAlexander, Hubert Horton.
    Strawberry Plains Audubon Center : four centuries of a Mississippi landscape / Hubert H. McAlexander.
        p. cm.
    Includes bibliographical references and index.
    ISBN 978-1-60473-002-9 (paper : alk. paper) 1. Strawberry Plains Audubon Center—History. 2. Wildlife refuges—Mississippi—Marshall County—History. 3. Nature centers—Mississippi—Marshall County—History. 4. Landscape—Mississippi—Marshall County—History.
5. Plantations—Mississippi—Marshall County—History. 6. Finley family.
7. Plantation owners—Mississippi—Marshall County—Biography.
8. Conservationists—Mississippi—Marshall County—Biography.
9. Marshall County (Miss.)—Biography. 10. Marshall County (Miss.)—History, Local. I. Title.
    QL84.22.M7M38 2008
    508.762'88—dc22

                                                2007045733

British Library Cataloging-in-Publication Data available

CONTENTS

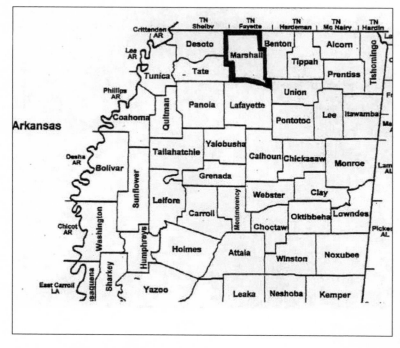

Map of northern Mississippi

FOREWORD

In 1982 sisters Ruth Finley and Margaret Finley Shackelford had wills drawn bequeathing 2500 acres and two antebellum houses in Marshall County, Mississippi, to the National Audubon Society. Ruth Finley died in 1984, and early in 1998 Margaret Shackelford relinquished her lifetime tenancy rights to the family home in Holly Springs, the county seat. The Audubon Society then opened its new state office headquarters there and also began working at Strawberry Plains, the plantation four miles north of the courthouse, where Mrs. Shackelford was living. After her death in the fall of 1998, the society took full possession of the sisters' bequest and established Strawberry Plains Audubon Center. The property lies one county east of the Mississippi River along the southern border of western Tennessee.

This book documents the rich and complex history of the 2500-acre tract encompassed by the Strawberry Plains Audubon Center. The cast of characters is wide and varied, representing six generations and three races that have been tied to and shaped by this land through the changing contours of history. In as far as possible, the story is told through their own words in documenting the personal histories, the built environment, and the changing cultural and economic conditions of life on this landscape.

Because so many people figure in this history and their relationships are intertwined, readers may want to consult often the genealogies in Appendix A. The maps in the front pages will help readers keep their bearings geographically throughout the narrative.

ACKNOWLEDGMENTS

Were it not for Strawberry Plains Audubon Center's director, Madge Lindsay, who felt the need for such a history, this book would not have been undertaken. And were it not for the enthusiastic support of Paul Calame, Nancy Fant Smith, and Carlyle Blakeney, advisors to the Shackelford Trust, it could never have been completed as expeditiously as it has been.

I have known this landscape and its people all my life and collected bits of its history for much of that span. But to give the full picture, a great deal of additional research was necessary—in archives, public records, family genealogies, historical treatments of the region and state, and oral history projects. For coming to my aid untold times, I wish to thank Bobby Mitchell, who shared with me his knowledge of the Civil War in the county and who so generously pursued other leads for me and provided copies of documents that I needed. The historian of Strawberry Plains Missionary Baptist Church, Willie Hayes Mallory, and I have enjoyed pursuing converging interests and sharing the results of our research. It has been a stimulating and rewarding interchange. Chelius H. Carter, Benton Cox, Lester G. Fant III, Lemuel A. Smith III, Dr. Carol Anderson, Steve Caviness, Prof. Barbara McCaskill, Prof. Frances Nicol Teague, Lauren Whitfield Ray, Dr. Robert Emmon Tyson, the Rev. Dr. Milton Winter, Dr. Charles Hudson, Edward Stephenson McAlexander, and Dr. Harvey Ouzts also have my gratitude.

Prof. David Coffey of the History Department at Virginia Military Institute was a gracious and informed guide to Rockbridge County, Virginia, as was Ruth Anne Agnor Herring, who provided me with material about Rockbridge architecture and took me through the Greenlee house once known as Clover Hill, which she then owned. The Lyle van Ravenswaays, who have beautifully restored the Greenlee's Ferry house, were my hosts for a wonderful morning at this place that I had heard about for so many years, and their daughter Lisa was particularly helpful in assembling information for me.

I thank the cooperative and efficient people who aided and expedited my research at all the archives in which I worked, including the Wisconsin State Historical Society, Madison, Wisconsin; Leyburn Library at Washington and Lee University; Alderman Library at the University of Virginia; the Tennessee State Library and Archives; the Mississippi Department of Archives and History (especially Grady Howell); and the John Davis Williams Library, University of Mississippi. I was particularly fortunate that the most extensive and most important holding, the Audubon Mississippi/Strawberry Plains Finley Collection at the University of Mississippi, is under the supervision of Jennifer Ford, Head of Special Collections, who extended me every courtesy and was unfailingly generous, concerned, and supportive throughout the project. Another repository where I have spent many hours is the Marshall County Chancery Clerk's Office in Holly Springs, and I wish to thank the staff there.

As I approached the Civil War chapters, I was fortuitously contacted by Dr. Patricia Swan, who was assisting her husband, Dr. James Swan, on research for his history of the 90th Illinois Regiment. One of the joys of this book was the triangular email exchange over several months conducted by Pat Swan, Bobby Mitchell, and me as we swapped information, pursued clues, and shared hunches in an effort to uncover the history of the military campground on the Coldwater River. This stimulating experience was a model of what communal scholarly research can be.

I was fortunate, too, that as I began the book, the Strawberry Plains/Audubon Mississippi Oral History Project (supported in part by the Mississippi Humanities Council) had just concluded two years of fieldwork interviewing a variety of people connected with the Finley family and the lands they controlled, with a concentration upon former sharecroppers and other renters during the period 1920 to 1960. For providing me timely access to the transcriptions, I am obliged to Dr. David Wharton of the Center for the Study of Southern Culture at the University of Mississippi, director of the project, and to Dr. Stephen Sloan, codirector of the Center for Oral History and Cultural Heritage at the University of Southern Mississippi, where the interviews were transcribed and are now housed. This valuable resource exists because of the efforts of Dr. Phillip Ensley, who volunteered his time in planning and finding grant funds for the project.

In assembling information on various families of the Strawberry Plains neighborhood, I called a number of times on the genealogical research skills of Ellnora Lancaster Rose Young, the great-great-granddaughter of Eliza Stephenson, who fearlessly ran the blockade with Martha Greenlee Davis. I profited from Dr. Lillian Wilson Stratmon's knowledge of the dramatic success story of her great-grandfather Holmes Teer. Professor Seth Yarborough Young generously put at my disposal his excellent work on the Davis family in Virginia and North Carolina. For information on the Eben Nelms Davis family, I had access to family material collected by his great-granddaughter Mary Ann Stanback Wilson. Mrs. Wilson, her sister Josephine Stanback Jones, and cousin Nell Fitts Beswick also shared with me memories and impressions of family members going back many decades—in the case of Mrs. Beswick back to the early years of the last century.

I am happy to acknowledge the support of the Department of English, University of Georgia, in providing me the research assistance of J. Anderson Frazee. I had the pleasure of watching his immersion in the agricultural schedules of the U.S. census and in the records of the Freedmen's Bureau seep even into his poetry. At Strawberry Plains Audubon Center, staff members Mary Lynn Riley, Kristin Lamberson, and Chad Pope all welcomed my visits and shared their knowledge of the center's activities and its goals. At the end of the project, my experience with the University Press of Mississippi was made pleasant, easy, and stimulating through the good offices of Craig W. Gill.

Finally, I am grateful to Dean Hugh Ruppersburg for his encouragement and support. My editor for nearly forty years, Dr. Patricia Jewell McAlexander, merits again my special thanks for her rigorous but sympathetic editing.

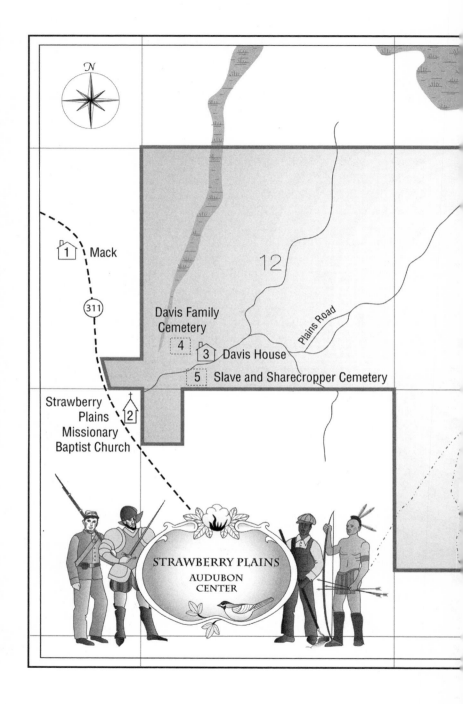

N

1 Mack

311

12

Davis Family
Cemetery

Plains Road

4

3 Davis House

5 Slave and Sharecropper Cemetery

Strawberry
Plains
Missionary
Baptist Church

2

STRAWBERRY PLAINS
AUDUBON
CENTER

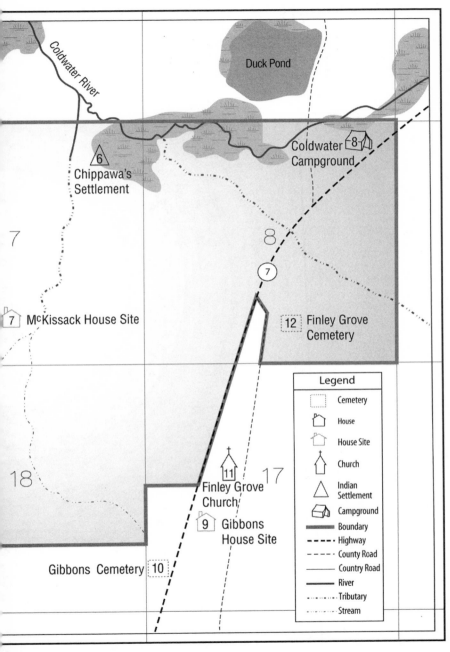

Map of Strawberry Plains Audubon Center. Drawing by Charlotte Ingram

STRAWBERRY PLAINS
AUDUBON CENTER

1

THE DEEP PAST

THE FIRST DOCUMENTED European explorers of the northern part of Mississippi arrived more than 450 years ago. In May 1539 an expedition led by Hernando de Soto, consisting of some 600 people, upward of 220 horses, a great herd of pigs, and numerous dogs, landed in Tampa Bay. A year and half later, after having taken a long and circuitous route through the southeastern United States, the Spanish expedition crossed the Tombigbee River, which snakes along the present-day eastern boundary of Mississippi down to the middle of the state. The Spaniards had entered the domain of the native people of Chicaza, later to be known as the Chickasaws, whom they easily defeated in battle. Noting that the fertile, well-cultivated land had produced an abundant storehouse of food, the conquistadors determined to spend the winter among their reluctant hosts. In early March 1541, offended and angered by de Soto's incessant demands, the people of Chicaza attacked the invaders just as they were preparing to depart, burning the Spanish barracks and killing twelve soldiers, fifty-seven horses, and hundreds of pigs. The Spaniards fought back, repaired their weapons, gathered supplies, and resumed their progress toward the northwest, through the largely uninhabited hunting grounds that include what would become Marshall County.[1]

Thus begins the legendary, misty first chapter in the recorded history of the tract of land from which the county would be formed. Centuries afterward, a tradition persisted that the Spanish conquistador had traveled through the county on his way to cross the Mississippi River south of the Chickasaw Bluffs at Memphis. The legend was given added credence by the discovery in 1901 of an ancient horseshoe at the center of a centuries-old oak on the Jarratt plantation on

Hernando de Soto. From
*Narratives of de Soto in
the Conquest of Florida*
(1866)

Spring Creek, five miles southeast of the present county seat, Holly Springs. Only in the final years of the twentieth century did archeologists who had studied the de Soto expedition establish that the party did indeed traverse Marshall County. So we are now free to picture the somewhat diminished but still great train of men and animals making its way across the mid-sixteenth-century landscape— the horsemen with cuirasses across the torso and carrying shields and long steel-pointed lances and the footmen armed with sharp, double-edged swords, or crossbows, matchlock gun, and halberds, all the adventurers wearing steel helmets.[2]

Concentrated in villages along the Tombigbee and Mississippi Rivers, the people of Chicaza were not only hunters and gatherers, but also agriculturists, as evidenced by the quantities of corn the Spaniards were so pleased to find. They lived in houses of mud-plastered logs and poles, most within villages. Beginning with these Spanish explorers, the descriptions of the tribe by soldiers, historians, and other travelers are uniformly respectful and admiring. "The nation of the Chickasaws is very warlike," wrote Le Page du Pratz in the 1720s. "The men have regular features, well shaped, and neatly dressed; they are fierce, and have a high opinion of themselves."[3]

By the end of the eighteenth century, the Chickasaw tribe was in a time of transition. There had been increasing contact with white American colonials, and African slaves had been introduced. The most prominent of the colonials to settle among the tribe was James Colbert, who had come into the domain as a youth in 1730, sired a large family by three Chickasaw wives, and by 1782 held 150 slaves. In 1790 Maj. John Doughty of the U.S. Army gave this report: "Of late years [the Chickasaws] have done less hunting than ever, for Want of Traders to purchase of them. They possess a great many Horses & some families have Negroes & Cattle. They live in Plenty in their Towns. Their Provisions [include] Hogs, Poultry, Eggs, Beans, Corn & the finest Potatoes I ever saw. The Chickasaws appear to be verging fast towards the State of Farmer. Game is getting scarce. [They] kill Bear, Otter, Deer, & some Beaver. The Chickasaws & Choctaws dress their skins to make them more valuable. They dispose of large Quantities of Bear Oil for the Orleans Markett [sic]." As the members of the tribe were becoming increasingly a farming people, they were also steadily establishing villages well to the north and west of the Tombigbee River, first in present-day Lee County, then in Pontotoc County, and by the end of the eighteenth century in Marshall County, which borders the state of Tennessee.[4]

The 1805 diary of Philadelphian Dr. Rush Nutt is the earliest source to document the Marshall settlement. "N.W. of Tallahatchee [River] in some rich prairies on a small clear running creek, called the pigeon roost," he noted, "many families of Indians have settled & are making good improvements. The country for many miles around there lays well for farming. Soil, fine dark & deep with a rich mould, clothed with black walnut, cherry, sugartree, maple, mulberry, oak & hickory, the low land covered with cane and peavine, the high land with sedge grass." Twenty years later this Pigeon Roost community was dominated by the Love family, founded by Thomas Love, a Tory who had fled into the Chickasaw domain at the end of the Revolutionary War and married into the Colbert dynasty. Located six miles southwest of the future site of Holly Springs, the settlement was so prosperously established that Presbyterian missionaries chose the place for a northern outpost of their missionary efforts. The new mission station was named Martyn, and a letter written from the station

"Characteristick Chicka-
saw Head" by Captain
Bernard Roman, 1771.
Reproduced in James H.
Malone, *The Chickasaw
Nation* (1922)

about 1830 by Miss Cornelia Pelham provides the first detailed description of a place in what is now Marshall County:

> In this letter I propose to give you a brief history of the missionary
> station of Martyn, under the superintendence of the Rev. Mr. Blair.
> The Indian name of the settlement in which this station is situated
> is *Pacha Noosa*, the English of which is *Pigeon Roost*. In the neigh-
> boring white settlements the people call it the *Love Village*, because
> many families by the name of Love reside there. There were in the
> school, at one time ten out of twenty-four scholars whose names
> were Love. . . . There are a considerable number of families of mixed
> blood, within two miles of the station; some of the members of the-
> ses families were educated in the mission school at Monroe. A black-
> smith's shop and grist mill show that civilization has made consid-

erable progress in the neighborhood. . . . Within six or eight miles
there are two full Indian settlements, which are pleasantly situated,
and make an unusually neat appearance. Many of the people living
in the vicinity of Martyn can understand English, and without the
aid of an interpreter. . . . [T]he buildings were commenced in the
latter part of 1825, but the school was not opened until August 1826.
When the establishment was completed, it was a comfortable place
and far from unpleasant. The houses were built of hewn logs, and
had brick chimneys, with convenient out-houses, and a garden con-
taining three quarters of an acre, enclosed by a suitable fence.

The first comprehensive map of the area, drawn in 1834, shows the
missionary station in the midst of Love farms. The largest farming
operation was that of Henry Love (son of Thomas), lying on the road
from Cotton Gin Port on the Tombigbee to Memphis. One of Love's
fields in Pigeon Roost bottom covered over a hundred acres.[5]

By this period, the powerful mixed-blood families were in ascen-
dancy in the Chickasaw nation. While the 1834 maps drawn for the
U.S. government indicate a number of mixed-blood settlements, few
full-blood villages are noted. Conspicuous among them is the settle-
ment of a man named Chippawa on the Strawberry Plains Audubon
Center tract. This Chickasaw full-blood is also mentioned in two
surviving memoirs of the period. In October 1831, Dr. Felix Grundy
Shipp left Hinds County, Mississippi, bound for Middle Tennessee;
he later recalled that on the nineteenth, "we ate breakfast at an old
Indians named Chippawa north of [the site of] Holly Springs on
Coldwater. . . . This creek old Chippawa told us the Indian name,
O'cocoppisah (English Coldwater). We [then] struck the white settle-
ments at LaGrange, Tenn." The Coldwater in Marshall County has
been called variously a creek or a river by both natives and visitors.
The phrase "on Coldwater" has been for many years a commonly
used localism. The wide flatland bordering the river north of the
Audubon Center land is known as Coldwater Bottom.[6]

A member of the pioneering Jarratt family also left a record of
this Chickasaw living on Coldwater, "There was in the old neighborhood . . . a small Indian settlement. Chippowie was the name of
the old chief. He owned negroes, and he was not at all savage looking, but rather of a mild appearing nature. On a near-by farm was a

negro man whose sole possession was a drum that was the pride and delight of his soul. Chippowie had a sick child raving with fever. He sent to borrow the drum to exorcise or frighten off the evil spirits afflicting the child. The negro was willing to accommodate his more ignorant neighbor, but he alone must carry the drum, and he alone could properly beat it." The Jarratt memoir reminds us of the early existence of three races in the region, the fact that two of them had enslaved the third, and it reveals a glimpse of the complex dynamic among the three.[7]

The completion of the 1834 maps was an important benchmark in the plan to move the Chickasaws west of the Mississippi. By the Treaty of Pontotoc, signed in October 1832, they had ceded their tribal lands in northern Mississippi to the United States. Then in the spring of 1834 before the mapping was completed, five Chickasaw leaders— one full-blood, two Colberts, and two Loves—traveled to Washington, D.C., to negotiate changes to the treaty. The entire tribe held in common the Chickasaw domain, and by the Treaty of Pontotoc proceeds from land sales were to go into a general fund, from which individuals received payment according to a formula based on family size and number of slaves owned. But in 1834 the tribal delegation won the concession that over one-third of the six million acres would be allotted directly to individual Chickasaws, who could then sell the land themselves, though only with approval of the Washington delegates and "King Ishtahotopa." The two treaties, which acknowledged Chickasaw economic realities, both protected less worldly tribesmen and placed the mixed-bloods in the position to make a great deal of money. The Chickasaw removal was not to be a trail of tears. Wealthy mixed-bloods had already traveled to Indian Territory (eventually Oklahoma) to find suitable cotton lands, where they could advantageously use their Mississippi profits.[8]

Two sites on what is now the Audubon tract became important during the period of white settlement and Indian removal. One of the locations considered in 1836 for the seat of the newly created county of Marshall was identified as simply "Shippowah." It was actually a foregone conclusion that the village at the "holly springs" would be chosen. Still, the remote possibility exists that the county seat could have been on the Audubon center tract, rather than five miles due south.[9]

Another site of greater significance in Chickasaw history lies approximately a mile east of Chippawa's village, on the headwaters of the Coldwater River at the extreme northeastern corner of the Audubon tract. Here, a natural camping ground was one of the primary points where tribesmen and their slaves from all over the Chickasaw nation were gathered for transport to Indian Territory. "I do not think that I have ever been a witness of so remarkable a scene," an observer commented:

> This immense column of moving Indians, several thousand, with the train of Gov' waggons [sic], the multitude of horses; it is said three to each Indian & beside at least six dogs & cats to an Indian. They were all most comfortably clad—the men in complete Indian dress with showy shawls tied in turban fashion round their heads—dashing about on their horses, like Arabs, many of them presenting the finest countenances & figures I ever saw. The women also very decently clothed like white women in calico gowns—but much tidier & better put on than common white-people—& how beautifully they managed their horses, how proud & calm & erect, they sat in full gallop. . . . It was a striking scene at night—when the multitudes of fires kindled showed to advantage the whole face of the country covered with white tents and white covered waggons, with all the interstices (between them) filled with a dense mass of animal life in the shape of savages, uncouth looking white hunters, the picturesque looking Indian negroes, with dresses belong to no country but partaking of all, & these changing & mingling with the hundreds of horses hobbled & turned out to feed & the troops of dogs chasing about in search of food—& then you would hear the whoops of Indians calling their family party together to receive their rations, from another quarter a wild song from the negroes preparing the corn, with the strange chorus that the rest would join in—& this would set a thousand hounds baying & curs yelping—& then the fires would catch tall dead trees & rushing to the tops throw a strong glare over all this moving scene.

Not all of the tribe left, however, and the Goforths, a mixed-blood family, continued to live to the north of the Chippewa village for another decade.[10]

But we are getting ahead of our story. By the summer of 1835, hundreds of Americans were coming into the Chickasaw Cession, an advance guard before the government land sales the following January. Many were connected with speculating land companies, some based as far away as New York and Boston. Others came from surrounding states or from the eastern seaboard looking for land to occupy and farm. The Chickasaw Cession was an unusual frontier, bordered on one side by the Mississippi River and on the other three by lands that had been opened to settlement from three to thirty years before. These adjacent regions were full of experienced frontiersmen, poised now to move into new territory beyond the sound of a neighbor's axe. The six million acres of the Chickasaw domain were widely advertised as "Cotton's last empire."[11]

In January 1836, the Chickasaw Cession land sales opened. Thousands now poured in. The land had been charted into sections (a one square mile unit of 640 acres), within townships (a gathering of thirty-six sections running north to south) and ranges (a gathering of thirty-six sections running east to west). The five sections of land comprising Strawberry Plains Audubon Center were all purchased on the first day of the sale by land speculators. By May 1836 the newly created county of Marshall had a population of 3100 "free" and 800 "colored" inhabitants. In July the newly elected country governing board, meeting in a rough log building overlooking the "holly springs," settled on plans for a court house in that village—a building forty-two by fifty-four feet, to rise two stories from a foundation of native rock (faced with a layer of cut stone "of a quality usual in Nashville, Louisville, or Cincinnati") to a domed octagonal cupola.[12]

The founding fathers had grand dreams. A female academy had already been established, a classical school for men would follow, and religious denominations had sent missionaries. The Chickasaws were still in evidence—the first group would not be removed to Indian Territory until June 1837, at which time the population of Marshall County numbered 13,498, of whom 8274 were white and 5224 were slaves. The count for Holly Springs stood at 1544. This was the setting when the first of the Finleys, the central figures in our large cast, entered the scene.[13]

2

THE FINLEYS

JOHN TATE FINLEY, the great-grandfather of the benefactors of Strawberry Plains Audubon Center, was born on November 13, 1801, in Augusta County, Virginia, the son of Samuel Finley and Mary Tate. Both the Finleys and the Tates were among the founding families of the Valley of Virginia, Ulster Scots (or Scotch-Irish), descended from Scottish Covenanters. Well-educated, though not college bred (only his younger brother William continued his education at Washington College in Lexington), John Finley in early manhood began farming some twenty miles from his birthplace in the southern reaches of Rockbridge County.[1]

His farm was in the Fancy Hill section, a post office that took its name from the oldest and largest of a group of imposing brick manor houses called The Seven Hills of Rockbridge: Fancy Hill, Fruit Hill, Rose Hill, Hickory Hill, Liberty Hill, Cherry Hill, and Clover Hill. These last two mansions were owned by an uncle and a brother of James Greenlee of Greenlee's Ferry near Natural Bridge, at whose home Finley began courting. The object of his attentions was Greenlee's daughter Mary Jane, whom he married on March 27, 1834. The ceremony was performed in the family home by the Rev. John D. Ewing, the minister at Falling Spring Presbyterian Church, where her family had worshiped for decades.[2]

Though not as imposing as the houses on the seven hills, the Greenlee's Ferry house was still a substantial brick manor, its front facade of rather Presbyterian austerity. The house was set on a knoll above the James River, situated between two spurs of the Blue Ridge Mountains; it was built in the last quarter of the eighteenth century by Mary Jane's grandfather and stood in the midst of a productive farm of 859 acres. This historic place, visited by Thomas Jefferson in

The Greenlee manor, Greenlee's Ferry, Rockbridge County, Virginia.
Courtesy of Lisa van Ravenswaay

1817, would many years later play a significant role in the fortunes of
the Mississippi Audubon Center lands.[3]

So, too, would ancestral tradition and genetic inheritance. The
source of both was Mary Jane's great-grandmother, a fabled figure
in the Valley of Virginia. The first white woman to enter that part
of the valley below Staunton, Mary McDowell Greenlee lived into
her ninety-eighth year. Fifty-two years a widow, she displayed great
ability in managing a large estate and left her children wealthy. She
was the daughter of Ephraim McDowell, who also lived to a great
age, and the great aunt of Dr. Ephraim McDowell, called the father
of abdominal surgery. Remembered as a beauty, Mary McDowell
Greenlee also possessed remarkable powers of mind, which she re-
tained until the end. Asked to state her age for a deposition taken
November 10, 1806, she snapped, "Ninety-five the 17th of this instant, and why do you ask me my age? Do you think that I am in my
dotage?" Her mental acuity and biting wit may account for her reputation as a witch in the folklore of the region, which resulted in this

bit of doggerel that has been passed down the years: "Mary Greenlee died of late / Straight she went to heaven's gate / But Abram met
her with a club / And knocked her down to Beelzebub." The family,
however, attributed any tales of evil repute to her youngest and favorite son, Samuel, who told a party of Methodist ministers bent
upon calling on the sturdy Calvinist that she had been burned at the
stake and a black cat found in her place. At any rate, her descendants
grew up with the tales of Mary's strength, daring, and tenacity. This
matriarch must have come many times to the minds of the Greenlee
girls later in Mississippi when they had their own experiences of frontier life, war, want, and bereavement. Not only was she an example to
follow, but her very blood may have given them their mettle.[4]

In March of 1834, Mary Jane Greenlee Finley, not yet twenty, was
having her golden day as a young bride. The couple moved to John
Finley's farm a few miles away, but by the end of the year Mary Jane
was back within the ancestral walls. There, on December 28, 1834,
she delivered her first child, George James (named for his father's
brother and his mother's father). It is he who would eventually lay
the groundwork for the Finley ownership of the Mississippi Audubon tract.[5]

By the time that Mary Jane and her son returned to the Finley farm, John Tate Finley was contemplating an autumn trip to
the south to explore possibilities for relocating. Many Virginians
were moving to newly opened territories, and Finley was drawn by
what a Virginian of his acquaintance called the "mania for Chickasaw
lands." He liked what he saw in the Chickasaw region and returned
intent upon moving. By the middle of June 1836, he, Mary Jane, and
their son were making their final round of visits before leaving for
Mississippi. Mary Jane was again pregnant, in her third month.[6]

In November 1836 her second child, Mary Virginia, was born in
Marshall County, Mississippi. John Finley had purchased a 680-acre
tract on Spring Creek less than three miles southeast of Holly Springs,
the village of log buildings now named the county seat of what was
being called "the Empire County." John Finley's earliest extant letter back to Virginia, headed "At Home near Holly Springs, Miss,
Feby 23rd 1837," is full of enthusiasm. He reports that he and Mary
Jane and the two children are flourishing. He has cleared and plowed

fifty acres and has his "cotton ground ready to bed up." He satirizes his own delight with the family's one-room log cabin: "Our House is vastly comfortable having a Hall, chamber & dining room—the whole lighted by one window—I have the only glass window in the neighborhood—& warmed by one fire—in short we are enjoying the enviable contentment which is only known to inmates of the cottage." Holly Springs, with a population of 1000, had prospects of a bank and a railroad to the Mississippi River, and these features will give it a "decided advantage over all of the towns in the Chickasaw Purchase in a commercial point of view, as it already has in population, wealth, intelligence, and respectability." Finally, he reports that Mary Jane "with all her predetermination not to be pleased has said more than once that she has been agreeably disappointed in the country & people."[7]

An important sign of further approval came six months later, on August 26, 1837, when Mary Jane moved her membership from the Falling Spring Presbyterian Church to the newly formed Presbyterian church in Holly Springs, becoming the eighteenth member on the roll. By that time, John Finley could report to Virginia relatives that some fine houses were under construction in the village, building was underway on a brick structure for the female academy to accommodate 100 students, and a movement had been launched to turn the male classical school into the first university in Mississippi. More than the material advances of this frontier, however, he was struck with spirit abroad in the new land, the "enterprise and energy among the people that you Virginians are strangers to."[8]

As fall approached, he had logs ready to build a "big log *House*, 22 feet square," which with the earlier cabin would allow the Finleys to accommodate visitors. Although the spring on the property "does well," he had also dug a well close to the house and had "fine water." The plantation had produced "a great amount of vegetables & some for sale," especially notable being vast quantities of sweet potatoes and watermelons. Both his corn and cotton crops were promising, and Finley estimated that he might harvest 1500 pounds of cotton to the acre.[9]

The next summer John Finley fulfilled a promise to Mary Jane and took her back to Virginia for a long visit. He used his time there to purchase more slaves, as well as equipment and supplies more readily available in an older region. By the middle of November 1838, John was writing back to Virginia that the Finleys had reached Marshall County after a trip of "23 days resting one." He joked that Mary Jane's new gold watch, acquired while at Greenlee's Ferry, had the result that she "evinces considerable more pride particularly on the subject of houses & that she, I really begin to think, considers it something near akin to degradation to live in a Mississippi scutch down with a wooden Chimney." Then he broke out, "Well confound the old cabin. I begin to hate it myself for it is not comfortable much now in any way we can fix it, for it is always *hot*, except when a northwester comes, then it is cold as vengeance." The dissatisfaction had reached its peak, when Mary Jane received a call from another native of Rockbridge County now settled in Holly Springs—the rather grand Mrs. Dr. Patrick Phillip Burton, nee Mary Malvina Shields of Lexington. John reported, "Mary Jane's pride was so much mortified that she declares she will leave the cabin when the very next folks visit." The long and short of the matter was that subsequently John supervised construction of "a kitchen, smoke house & nice building, none of your scutch downs but of nicely hewed logs & nailed roofs." He expected to be in "our new House" in a few days.[10]

Mississippi, like the rest of the nation, was still feeling the effects of the Panic of 1837, brought on in part by Andrew Jackson's Specie Circular, which required payment for public lands in gold or silver in an attempt to reduce the amount of paper money in circulation and limit land speculation. In addition, the 1838 cotton crop was about half the yield of the preceding year, but Finley was still convinced of the bright future of this new region. Editors of the two local newspapers echoed his enthusiasm in touting the county seat. "Is it not a beautiful village," effused the editor at the Holly Springs *Guard*, "with its spacious square and splendid Court House, with it neat Churches and Academies, with its fine rows of brick buildings for business, and its white cottages for comfort, with their gardens full of vines and evergreens, and flowers and fragrance when the breath of summer stirs them, and all so new and fresh, as if just sprung up from the wilderness, at the command of enchantment." The *Holly Springs Gazette* followed suit in the boosterism, though statistically, rather than lyrically: "In every respect Holly Springs is worthy of the Empire County. We number nineteen dry goods and produce stores, five church edifices, fifteen lawyers offices, six doctors shops, three taverns, two silversmiths shops, five blacksmiths, two hatters, and six tailors shops, two coach makers, two wagon makers, three boot and shoe shops, and an iron foundry, where plows and various other articles are cast." Finley felt that an investment in the village would be a wise one, and he joined in a partnership with prominent speculator William Cain and fellow Rockbridge County native Alexander T. Caruthers to purchase the most substantial of the town's three taverns, a colonnaded two-story building on the town square, the Union House.[11]

In June 1839 Finley began a letter to his brother-in-law James Dorman Davidson in Lexington by painting rather an idyllic scene: "We are all well and getting along a little after the Mississippi fashion— a fine season so far. Corn in the field in tassel, some cotton about blooming, fine oats & a *good meadow*—plenty of garden eatables— will have tomatoes plenty in a week." But grim realities soon intruded. "Times are hard," he admitted. Bankruptcies were common, so at least John's younger brother, the lawyer William Finley, who had also moved to Marshall, was busy. But a significant number of planters were emigrating to Texas.[12]

In the fall, the Union House was the setting for a grand dinner for Gen. Sam Houston, a native of the Valley of Virginia and cousin of both Mrs. Burton and business partner Alexander Caruthers. Toasts to the Republic of Texas were followed by Houston's speech to a huge crowd at the courthouse. Such memorable occasions were now few, and in January 1840 Finley wrote that cotton was selling at only half the price of the year before, and that "this County is debt ridden almost to death."[13]

On April 20, 1840, James Greenlee, at age seventy-two, drowned in the James River at Greenlee's Ferry. It was decided that the estate, which was also feeling the hard economic times, would be kept together to support his widow. John Finley wrote that he and Mary Jane

An 1854 ferrotype of the southeastern corner of the Holly Springs courthouse square, showing buildings erected in the 1830s, including John T. Finley's colonnaded Union House. The 1849 Methodist Church is in the background. The picture was sent by Samuel E. Carey to his parents in New York state, to whom he commented, "You can see by this exactly how the cotton is put up. These bales generally hold 500 lbs. . . . How natural those oxen look, the first you see, turning round, the mules too, standing half asleep." Courtesy of Henry Dancy

did not expect to realize anything from an immediate settlement, but he also expressed the hope that the Greenlee heirs would not be saddled with debt. The Finleys were careful people with money. Finley blamed Andrew Jackson for the country's financial difficulties, and the next year he ran successfully for the Mississippi legislature as a Whig.[14]

Five years after settling in the Chickasaw Purchase, John Tate Finley had established himself as one of the premier citizens of Marshall

County. A substantial planter, a significant investor in Holly Springs, a respected political figure, Finley had weathered the Panic of 1837 and the following depression. He never overextended himself financially; he kept what he had and steadily added to it. This would become a trait of the Finley line in Marshall.

3

THE DAVISES

IN 1843 MARY JANE FINLEY invited her twenty-year-old sister, Martha Trimble Greenlee, down for a long visit in Mississippi. On November 6 John Finley wrote James D. Davidson, "Martha has a beau who visits regularly a pretty clever Red headed red faced fellow, don't drink, all natural, produced by the reflection of his hair. She says he has made no [indecipherable] proposition. But one thing is certain, he is badly in for it." Finley predicted well. By the time of Martha's return, she and her suitor had reached an agreement, and on March 31, 1845, Finley reported to Davidson that Eben Nelms Davis had left ten days before for Virginia and "suppose by this time he is safely moored at Greenlee's Farm." On April 1 at the Greenlee manor, Martha was married to the forty-three-year-old widower from Marshall County by the same minister of Falling Spring Presbyterian Church who had married Mary Jane and John Finley eleven years before.[1]

Eben Nelms Davis had come to Marshall County in 1837 and purchased from a land speculator Section 12, Township 3, Range 3, the westernmost tract in what is now the Strawberry Plains Audubon Center. Born in North Carolina, he was the son of Willie Jones Davis and Elizabeth Nelms. Willie (pronounced Wiley) Davis, who moved from the Old North State to Williamson County in Middle Tennessee before 1820, appears to have been only moderately successful, though there was some money in his background—his mother was Winifred Duke, daughter of a wealthy man. Elizabeth Nelms traced herself back to Peter Presley (d. 1693), member of the Virginia House of Burgesses from Northumberland County. Presley's daughter Elizabeth married Ebenezer Saunders, and their grandson Presley

Nelms was Elizabeth Nelms Davis's father. These family names were continued among Davis descendants. Elizabeth named her son for her brother Eben Nelms (the full form Ebenezer had been shortened over time), who was a man of substance, generous to his namesake.[2]

The letters of Eben Nelms Davis, like those of John Tate Finley, reveal that he had received more than a solid "English education" (that is, basic training in arithmetic, reading, and writing) and that he had acquired the polish of a gentleman. He had also married well the first time. Susan Sills, whom he wed in 1830 in Nash County, North Carolina, was the daughter of David Sills, who provided generously for her in his will three years later.[3]

Shortly after Eben Davis purchased his Marshall County plantation in November 1837, he brought down his aged parents and his young, pregnant wife Susan. A son, David, was born in March 1838. Susan died two weeks later, and David succumbed after five months. It was a sad beginning for Eben's new life. Both were buried in properly marked graves in the cemetery in Holly Springs, and the bereaved husband and father set to work clearing his plantation four miles north off Mt. Pleasant Road. By the time that Eben Davis met Martha Greenlee in 1843, he had prospered and proven himself indeed to be "a pretty clever" fellow. Six months after the marriage, he purchased an additional 320 acres adjoining his land in the northern half of Section 7, a purchase that included the site of Chippawa's village. He now owned almost a thousand acres.

Just a few months before, the noted agriculturalist Solon Robinson had made a trip through Marshall County and left the first description of the landscape covered by the Davis plantation and the present Strawberry Plains Audubon Center tract. "This, 9th of Feb., four miles south of Lagrange [Tennessee], upon a very warm sunny day," he wrote,

> I crossed the Mississippi line. The grass to-day looks green and spring like, and plum trees are leaving and peach buds are just ready to burst into blossom. Much land shows that there has been a good deal of a kind of work done that people really seem to be in sober earnest when they call it "plowing." The weather is more like May

than February. Birds and frogs making melody—grass growing—
flowers blooming—gardens making, etc.

From here to Holly Springs, the county seat of Marshall co. [sic],
and a flourishing fine town, the land grows hilly and sandy, and bottom lands more swampy. The upland timber mostly black oak, inter-
spersed with white oak and hickory, much of it uncultivated. Some
fine farms.

The Eben Davis plantation certainly belonged in that category, and
five years later the agricultural schedules of the census listed it as having 610 "improved" acres and 350 "unimproved."[4]

Eben Davis's letters to James D. Davidson do not give the detailed
picture of frontier life provided by the Finley letters. But fortunately
we have the remarkable account, during the same time period, by a
tutor on a nearby plantation comparable to the plantation to which
Davis brought Martha Greenlee. Seymour Carpenter, later a physi-
cian and lieutenant colonel in the Union Army, was in 1846 an intel-
lectual young man of twenty who had just completed an education
at Granville College in Ohio. Determined to start life as a schoolmaster, he took a steamboat south to Memphis and was soon hired
by Maj. John H. Clopton of Marshall County to teach his children
and those of neighboring planters Col. William Clayton and Judge
William McAlexander. The Clopton plantation was located just three
miles northwest of Eben Davis's land.[5]

Because this was Carpenter's first exposure to a clime and culture
so different from his own, he left a painstaking portrait. The Clopton
house, he tells us, "was a large double, hewed-log house, a story and a
half high, with a twenty-foot space between the buildings, the whole
under the same roof, with a shed roof extending back of each of the
buildings, where the house was only one story. There were four large
rooms below, and two above, and the wide hall, where the family sat
most of the time. The building was whitewashed, and stood in a park
of fine trees, about twenty acres in extent." Carpenter then describes
the whole plantation grouping: "Off to one side, about a hundred
yards distant, were the negro cabins, about twenty in number; within
fifty feet was the kitchen, a large cabin about twenty feet square. Back
of the main building, about fifty yards distant, and the same distance

from each, were hewed-log houses, one story high." Carpenter comments that each slave family had a cabin, with a small vegetable garden attached. In addition to all the features forming the Clopton plantation configuration, the Davis plantation now also had a family burying ground. Eben Davis's mother, who had died in 1842, was the first to be buried in the plantation cemetery, set on a high bluff above the branch of the Coldwater River that ran through the western edge of the Davis tract.[6]

The Clopton family consisted of the major and his wife and eight children, as well as his father and spinster sister. The Cloptons and six of their children occupied the main house, his father and sister lived in one of the two one-story log houses, while Carpenter, the two oldest sons, and the overseer lived in the other. Apparently Martha Greenlee Davis found a much similar arrangement at the Davis plantation—in that case, two log houses, one built for Eben and his first wife and one for his parents. Carpenter's description of the interior of the main Clopton residence gives a sense of the Davis accommodations as well, "comfortably furnished, there being many old mahogany pieces, including a sideboard, and two four-post bedsteads, with canopies, which occupied one of the large front rooms, that served as a guest chamber, as well as a parlor. The bedspreads and pillows in this show-room were profusely embellished with ruffles. There were no carpets or rugs. Several large mirrors adorned the walls." At the Eben Davis place, there were no doubt a few Davis and Sills pieces, to which Martha added purchases from Holly Springs cabinet makers.[7]

Eben Davis's nearest neighbors were the Stephenson and Williams families. Maj. Josiah Patrick Milledge Stephenson had come to Marshall among the first wave of settlers, purchasing his place in 1836. His was the smallest of the immediate plantations, occupying the eastern half of Section 11 adjoining the Davis land on the west. In addition to growing cotton, he also operated what became to be one of the largest nurseries in the Middle South, an 1846 newspaper noting that he had ten thousand fruit trees for sale. The Stephenson log house was only half a mile from the Davis complex at a sweeping curve of the Holly Springs–Mt. Pleasant road, created in 1840 when the county governing board ordered that the major "be allowed to change the [road] around his garden." The Stephensons were a Scotch-Irish Presbyterian family hailing from Iredell County in the North Carolina piedmont (the same family that produced in a branch that changed the spelling of the name Vice-President Adlai Ewing Stevenson). The major's wife, Eliza Mitchell, descended from Southside Virginia stock, one line being the Jones clan of the Revolutionary aristocrat-democrat Willie Jones. The Stephensons had five children, including a daughter who would eventually be counted among Martha Davis's closest friends.[8]

The Williamses were the latest—and the grandest—of the settlers coming to Marshall. Benjamin W. Williams was the scion of a landed North Carolina family. His wife, Eliza, was possibly even better connected, having been born a Perkins, one of the wealthiest and most inbred families of Middle Tennessee. The banks of the Harpeth River were lined with their great brick mansions. The daughter of cousins Samuel Fearn Perkins and Sarah Leah Perkins, Eliza was born in 1813 in one of these mansions, West View, in Williamson County. In 1831 she married, naturally enough, her cousin Thomas Hardin Perkins, son of the union of another two Perkins cousins, whose great house was named Meeting of the Waters. Eliza and Thomas were married only two years before his death. The union produced one child, a son and namesake. In 1839 the widow Eliza married Benjamin W. Williams, and two years afterward they moved to Marshall County, where the Perkins family had already bought a large tract of land. Many of the slaves the Williamses brought were Perkins slaves. Benjamin Williams purchased a thousand acres adjoining the Davises and Stephensons, and he built not another log structure, but the first frame residence in the neighborhood, a one-and-a-half-story plantation house. Eliza would have settled for no less, and when her house was completed, she supervised the landscaping including the planting of a magnolia tree on either side of the front portico. She was a woman of fashion, cut from the same cloth as Mrs. Dr. Phillip Patrick Burton, whose visit to the Finley cabin had so embarrassed Mary Jane Finley.[9]

In a letter written back to Virginia, John Finley noted that Ben Williams, who stood bond on a note involving Greenlee business, "is I suppose the wealthiest man in the county." Then he added judicious praise from a Finley, commenting that Williams was "most independent not being in debt I mean no debts owing that are due— besides he is economical & prudent, a staunch Whig." The prominence, sound economic state, and civic-mindedness of Williams and of Eben Davis are indeed reflected by that the fact that both were numbered among the board of trustees of the fledgling University of Holly Springs in 1843.[10]

Three days before the Greenlee-Davis marriage in 1845, Benjamin and Eliza Williams deeded ten acres in the northwest corner of Section 10 to a Methodist meeting house, Wesley Chapel. The church that was soon built—a small frame building entered by two doors at the gable end, the interior plastered and furnished with finished pews—was located halfway between the Cloptons and the Davises. The congregation had been established in 1837, and among the early members were the Cloptons, Ben Williams, and Eben Davis. Eliza Perkins Williams was an Episcopalian and never joined, and Martha Davis must have found it difficult to leave the fold of John Calvin, but finally capitulated several years after marriage. The Clopton schoolmaster sketched well the importance of this church in the neighborhood in the mid-1840s:

Sunday was a great day; all, old and young, white and black, went to church. The ponderous carriage was brought out, which carried the old gentleman, Mrs. and Miss Clopton, and some of the smaller children. The Major and the rest of us, went on horseback; the negroes walked in a procession, headed by one of the oldest, who carried a written pass, allowing them to go, and return, from church. The Church building was two miles away, and if the day was fair there would be a large congregation, sometimes as many as fifteen or twenty carriages, for every planter of any standing had one. And the woods were full of horses and swarmed with colored people. They were not allowed in the church, but back of the pulpit was a large window which had only a shutter; in fact, none of the windows were glazed, and the colored people occupied rude benches on the outside of the building, where they could hear, but not see very much. Before and after service there was much visiting among the old folks, and a great deal of flirting among the younger ones. Occasionally

the Major would take guests home to dinner, or would himself dine
with some of his friends.

Seymour Carpenter comments later that the slaves were allowed to
raise and sell chickens, and "in that way got money to buy Sunday
clothes." On Sunday, most were "fairly well dressed."[11]

By 1846, just ten years after the opening of the Chickasaw Purchase, families were well settled on the land and institutions and patterns of life had been established. The major work of clearing the
land was over, and many a Marshall County neighborhood was centered on its church and its school. The little Methodist chapel was
not the Falling Spring Presbyterian Church, but society was good;
and Eben Davis would soon build for his family a mansion that com-
pared well with those in Rockbridge County, Virginia.

4

WOODLAND AND STRAWBERRY PLAINS

THE AVERAGE LIFE SPAN was considerably shorter in the nineteenth century than it is now, and infant mortality and a mother's
death in childbirth were alarmingly common. By 1842 Eben Davis
had already suffered the deaths of his first wife, his son, and his
mother. While he was away in Virginia for his second wedding, his father died and was buried beside Eben's mother in the family graveyard. Martha Greenlee Davis had become pregnant soon after her
marriage, and she bore a son in January 1846, but the child, Willie
Greenlee Davis, died before his second birthday. Early in 1847, Davis's neighbor, friend, and contemporary Ben Williams died at the
age of forty-six and was buried near his house. Eliza Williams marked
her husband's grave with a towering twelve-foot monument, and inspired by her example, Eben Davis placed a similar monument in
the Davis family cemetery and had inscribed on it the names of his
mother, his father, and his son Willie.

More shocking than any of these deaths, however, was one that
came the next spring. On April 31, 1848, Eben Davis wrote to his
brother-in-law James Dorman Davidson in Virginia: "It now be-
comes my duty as a friend & Brother to announce to you the death of
our Brother-in-law John T. Finley Esq. He departed this life with res-
ignation to the will of Heaven on the 27th Instant, leaving a berieven
[sic] family to mourn his irreparable loss." Davis reported that John
Finley died without a will but that, not surprisingly, "his estate was
entirely unencumbered." Eben Davis assumed that Mary Jane would
administer the estate and assured Davidson that "William Finley &
myself will assist her in all matters necessary."[1]

John Finley's estate papers provide excellent evidence of the circumstances of a substantial planting family of Marshall County in

the late 1840s. Finley died possessed of a 680-acre plantation, an undivided one-third interest in the Union House on the Holly Springs square, and thirty-four slaves. His stock consisted of eight mules, one bay mare, three horses, "four yoke of Steers," five cows and calves, fifty-two hogs, and thirty-six sheep. He owned a buggy, two wagons, and a horse cart. Plantation equipment and stores included a hundred barrels of corn, a stack of fodder and oats, fifteen bushels of rye, one corn sheller and cutting knife, one lot of farming utensils and shop tools, a grind stone, a thresher, a gin stand, one crusher, 1400 pounds of bacon and 150 pounds of lard, one lot of bagging and ropes, one steelyard, a supply of salt, two spinning wheels, and 28 pounds of wool. The contents of the plantation house and their value are of especial interest:

Two feather beds $40 each including Stead & Furniture	$80.00
Three beds, steds & Furniture $35.00 each Trunnel at 2.50	107.50
6 Cane bottom chairs 2.00 each 18 plain chairs 20 cts	15.60
one Rocking chair 2.50 Lot Table ware 12.00	14.50
Silver Spoons $18.00 Safe and contents $15.00	33.00
Folding table $6.00 one ditto $12.00 two small tables 4.50	22.50
one table 1.00 one china press $15.00	16.00
2 pair Andirons 1.50 each Small balances 1.00	4.00
Teaboard 50 cts lot Books 15.00 wardrobe 15.00	30.50
Bureau 20.00 Looking glass 2.00 2 candlesticks 1.50	23.50
2 washstands 5.00 Leather & kegs 5.00	10.00
Sugar & coffee $20.00 Barrel flour 5.00 Bag flour 2.50	27.50
Demijohn 1.50 candles 2.50 3 pair Sheep Shears .75 each	6.25
Saddle Bags 2.00 two guns 18.00 Closet contents 5.00	25.00
Two Atlases 6.00 55 lb Iron at 6 cts 3.30	9.30
Kitchen furniture 25.00 Lot of Jars 2.10 pair Balances 5.00	32.10

This inventory does not list items belonging to Mary Jane Greenlee Finley, which would have included her dowry of linens and china, her fine gold watch, and the baby bed brought from Virginia (now in the northeast bedroom of the Davis House at the Audubon Center). The inventoried furnishings suggest a house of four rooms and a detached kitchen. Like the Clopton house, floors were bare and the parlor likely also served as a bed chamber.[2]

Mary Jane Greenlee Finley (1814–1885) during the long years of her widowhood. Courtesy of the Audubon Mississippi/Strawberry Plains Finley Collection, University of Mississippi

Mrs. Finley was left with five children, George James (at the time of his father's death, a boy of thirteen), Mary Virginia (eleven), Emma Frances (eight), Augusta Caroline (six), and John Samuel (three years). John Finley had hired an overseer a month before his death, and the family would continue to retain various men in that position, even after the elder son assumed management of the family interests. The 1850s were the golden age in the cotton South, and thus the great period of building. Sometime during that decade, Mary Jane Finley replaced her log dwelling with a frame plantation cottage. Within the decade, the plantation was also given the name Woodland, quite probably by her daughters. During the nearly forty years of her widowhood, she remained on the plantation to assure that it be run smoothly and profitably.

At the time of John Finley's death, Eben and Martha Davis had already made plans for building a large brick residence, which was to be the largest plantation house yet erected in the county. On June 26,

1848, Davis paid Benjamin Davenport for the burning of seventy-five thousand bricks. The house to be constructed from them would not be built for three years, due either to economic circumstances or simply failure to secure the right builder. But Martha Greenlee Davis now knew that she was to have a manor house like those in Virginia on her plantation, which she had named Strawberry Plains.[3]

The Greenlee sisters had grown up in a country surrounded by the mansions of the Seven Hills, and the naming of Martha's Mississippi plantation must have been partly inspired by her uncle's Clover Hill. In the twentieth century, her granddaughter would speak of the native strawberries that her grandparents found in abundance on the tableland (or plains) of the plantation. Several historical sources confirm the presence of these strawberries in the southern states. James Adair's *History of the American Indians* (actually a history of the southern Indians) published in London in 1775, commented that the Indian "old fields abound with larger strawberries than I have seen in any part of the world; insomuch, that in the proper season, one may gather a hat-full, in the space of two or three yards square." William Bartram's *Travels* (1791), a treasure trove of botanical lore of the southeastern United States, notes wild strawberries at varied locales from South Carolina through Georgia and into Alabama. Writing in 1803, F. A. Michaux noted, "wild strawberry vines matted the earth where there were barrens; the ripe berries covered the ground as with a red cloth." According to the historian of the Chickasaws, James H. Malone "in the months of April and May strawberries were found profusely scattered amid the grass of the undulating prairies that lay along the banks of the rivers and creeks, and here and there scattered amid the hills and valleys of the forests." Martha Greenlee Davis must have been entranced by the sight, and the enchanting name she bestowed on the plantation is a part of the charm that has assured its preservation.[4]

In 1850 Eben Davis owned sixty-two slaves, almost twice the holding of the Finleys. He had cleared and was farming 610 of his 960 acres. Economic prospects were bright, and that year Marshall County led the state in cotton production. Within a short fourteen years, it had become a major agricultural center. By the spring of 1851,

Martha Trimble Greenlee
Davis (1823–1906) in her
early married life. Cour-
tesy of the Audubon
Mississippi/Strawberry
Plains Finley Collection,
University of Mississippi

Davis had hired the carpenters to complete his house. His son John
Presley, born October 23, 1851, was fond of saying that he and the
house were the same age.[5]

The structure that the Davises occupied at the end of 1851 was
the most substantial plantation house in the region. Set high off the
ground, the square brick mass, inspired by the Federal architecture
of Rockbridge County, rose two and a half stories. In the center of
the front facade was a narrow portico supported by four wooden
columns. The house was entered through double doors framed by
transom and sidelights. Above, opening onto an upper gallery, was a
single door framed similarly. At the end of the wide downstairs hall
rose a handsome balcony stair. On the left of the hall were double parlors joined by pocket doors. On the right front was a guest chamber,
and behind it the dining room with an outside door opening onto a
covered brick walk that led to a kitchen forty feet back of the mansion, as was the practice to keep smells and heat from the main house.
The second floor contained a hall and four large bedrooms, and the
third floor was one great room that served as the children's playroom
and nursery in mild weather.

The mansion at Strawberry Plains as it looked in 1851. Drawing by
Chelius H. Carter

It was a manor built and appointed for both complete comfort
and gracious living. The parlors were furnished with matching sets—
low sofa, a rocking chair, six Empire side chairs, and an Empire card
table. The front parlor also contained a square rosewood piano. There
were probably as many as eight bedsteads to accommodate family and
guests. Among the final purchases for the house were more than two
hundred yards of Brussels carpet, fifteen yards of stair carpeting, and
thirty yards of oilcloth floor covering.[6]

The house was set in a high, level park-like expanse amid ancient
red oaks (one of which survived until 2004, a towering specimen
with a high, broad-spreading canopy). In the midst of these native
oaks and hickories, Mrs. Davis had planted on the lawn in front of
the mansion as many as fifty red cedars—two rows to form an avenue
leading from the front portico to the road, and this central avenue
bisected by other rows of cedars. The wildlife—squirrels, birds of all

kinds, and butterflies—attracted by the cedars and oaks, the flowers and shrubs, created an idyllic air.[7]

By 1859 Martha Davis had borne eight children, three of whom had died in infancy. The great brick house was home to five children: Eben Nelms Jr. (b. 1847), John Presley (b. 1851), Mary Elizabeth (b. 1853), Ann Winifred (b. 1856), and Augusta Virginia (b. 1859). By the mid-1850s, Eben Davis had a large frame schoolroom constructed west of the house and hired a governess, who also instructed some other children of the neighborhood.

Like all large southern plantations, Strawberry Plains was, as far as possible, a self-sustaining unit. The overseers hired by Eben Davis likely lived in the original log house, which might have also been used as the plantation office. The log slave cabins for the house servants stood across the ravine on the ridge south of the main house, as did the slave cemetery. Cabins for the field hands stood on the eastern and northwestern reaches of the property. The plantation grouping was completed by a brick smoke house, a blacksmith's shop, a carriage house, barn, cotton gin, dairy, potato house, and an ice house located beside the pond to the northwest, its walls insulated with sawdust.[8]

Martha Davis had experienced her share of sorrow, but she remembered with great pleasure her school days in Lexington and the parties and dances in Rockbridge. She made sure that her children would have similar memories. Strawberry Plains had its own slave musicians. Her carriage, pulled by a matched pair of fine horses named Romulus and Remus, was kept ready to take her for visits in the neighborhood, in town, or most frequently to Woodland to visit Mary Jane and her children.

Though the standard of living at Woodland did not match that of Strawberry Plains, still the Finleys lived well. Good Presbyterian that she was, Mary Jane Finley saw to it that her children received a sound education. Holly Springs was particularly noted for its schools for women, and Virginia, Augusta, and Emma all graduated from the Holly Springs Female Institute, the school chartered before the town had even been laid out. George and John were sent with their cousin Sam (son of lawyer William Finley) to St. Thomas Hall, an Episcopal boys school founded in 1844.[9]

Two of Martha Davis's daughters, Emma (who died in infancy) and Augusta Virginia, were named for their Finley cousins, and the 1858 diary of her niece Emma Finley reveals the constant interaction between the two families. Martha's carriage, with her driver Edmund in command, was frequently transporting people between the two plantations. There was also much visiting back and forth with the kin in Virginia.

The Greenlee ties were strong. Eben Davis discovered that ten years after his marriage, when his wife and Mrs. Finley came forward to save their youngest brother from financial ruin. The note signed by Eben Davis and Mary Jane Finley was eventually secured against the James Greenlee estate at Greenlee's Ferry and led to complications in the settling of that estate for many years. But the Greenlees stood firm in coming to the aid of their own. That resolve would eventually be an initial cause behind the Finley family's accumulation of the acreage forming the Strawberry Plains Audubon Center tract.[10]

5

THE SLAVES

Accoording to the 1860 slave schedules of the U.S. census, E. N. Davis at Strawberry Plains in Marshall County owned 114 slaves. The census taker came on July 16, when field hands were cultivating the crops, and the slave count is divided into four sections: 16 house servants and skilled workers; 45 children under the age of thirteen; 27 male field hands, ages thirty to thirteen, and 26 female field hands, ages thirty-four to thirteen.[1]

That particular day the slave children would have been under the care of a mature nurse and several older slave girls. These nurses would have been included among the eleven female slaves in the group of house servants and skilled workers. Others of the eleven women servants, who ranged in age from fifty-four to sixteen, filled the positions of cook for the family and the house servants, cook for the field hands, housekeeper, house maid, laundress, and head nurse for the children of the big house. The five males in this first group, varying in age from sixty to twenty-five, would typically have included a blacksmith, a carpenter, a carriage driver who probably also oversaw the stables, a gardener, and a servant with general duties inside the big house. The names of only a few of these servants have been passed down. Aunt Sarah was the big house cook, Aunt Margaret Lee was the Davis children's nurse, her husband Frank Lee was a house servant, and Edmund was the carriage driver.[2]

The house servants were considered the privileged group among the slaves. They were the best dressed, and they ate the more varied and delicate fare that was served to the family. Some, in violation of Mississippi's slave laws, were taught to read by Martha Greenlee Davis. They lived on the ridge across the ravine from the front of the big house. According to the testimony of slaves on comparable Marshall County plantations, all slave dwellings were like the Finley's frontier cabin, "good log houses, with dirt and stick chimneys." Beds were what the slaves called one or two-legged "aggies" with one end fastened to the log walls. Mattresses were "pretty comfortable, with ticks stuffed with shucks and rye." These houses across the ravine, together with the clusters of cabins for field hands to the northwest and to the east, numbered twelve buildings. Some were one-room affairs, but married couples with a number of children were given double-pen log houses. Large planters typically set aside space by the slave cabins for small vegetable gardens. We know that, at Wood-cote plantation nearby, a patch was provided in the rear of the cabins for the slaves to grow tobacco for their own use. Many of the slave yards there also had chicken houses, and, at the neighboring Clopton plantation, "the thrifty women sold many chickens and eggs—thereby making their 'change.'"[3]

Census records reveal the identities of two of Eben Davis's overseers: in 1850 William A. Andrews, a twenty-six-year-old Alabamian, and in 1860 Booker Flippin, a twenty-four-year-old Virginian and the first cousin of neighboring planter Richard O. Woodson. Among the Strawberry Plains papers is Davis's contract with Flippin, a rare surviving document in northern Mississippi:

Article of an agreement made & entered into by & between E. N. Davis of the first part and Booker Flippin of the second part. To wit I Booker Flippin of the second part hath agreed to attend to the business of E. N. Davis as an Overseer for twelve months. I give my entire service to the said Davis for the said specified time. I agree to stay with & attend faithfully to the hands & see that their work is properly done. To treat the slaves as humanely & kind as their conduct will allow. To attend to the stock of every kind to see that they are properly fed and salted regularly. To attend to all the geare and tools of every kind to keep them in good order and in their proper places. To attend to the slaves & see that they have the proper attention on the part of the other servants. See that they keep their bedding and wearing apparel in good order, washed & mended & observe that each slave shall keep their person cleanly and hair combed once a week. I agree to attend to all the business appertaining to the duties of an Overseer & farthermore [sic] agree to make up or

Typical Marshall County slave cabin. Courtesy of the Dean Collection, University of Mississippi

deduct all loss time either by sickness or otherwise. Said Davis agrees on his part if the said Flippin shall continue with him for twelve months as agreed to do the said Davis is to pay said Flippin four hundred dollars at the rate of thirty-three dollars 33/100 cents per month & if either party shall become dissatisfied we can separate by the said Davis paying said Flippin for the time he may have been in service. Given under our hands Jany 17th 1860.

　　E. N. Davis
　　B. Flippin

Serving immediately under the overseer would have been one or more slave foremen (or drivers). The overseer's contract begins to convey to us some of the reality of chattel slavery, and the strange status of these human beings who were also regarded as possessions, like the stock and the tools.[4]

Flippin commenced his job soon after the harvest. As is true of all farming operations, work at Strawberry Plains had a seasonal rhythm. The first three months of the year were devoted to maintenance and repair and indoor work. Each slave "had his own task," Callie Gray, a former slave on the Fant plantation west of Holly Springs, told a WPA interviewer. "Some hauled wood to last all the year, some plaited corn-shuck mule collars, and split rails and mended fences and bottomed chairs and lots of other things." Some women, she said, "sewed all the time after Miss Liza cut out the clothes, and they sewed with they fingers 'cause they warn't no sewing machines. They spun the thread and dyed and wove it too. They dyed it with walnuts and shumake and oak bark, and copperas wus put in the dye too."[5]

From late March through late April, field hands were engaged in planting corn, oats, wheat, and vegetable gardens, as well as cotton. From late spring until August, hands labored cultivating the crops. "August," as one Marshall County resident recalled, "was a transition month—too soon to harvest and too late to plant or cultivate— a time to rest if such were possible in the heat and humidity." Another upland man who had himself labored in the cotton fields left a more lyric description of August: "It gave us a fine feeling to look out over our well-tilled fields and to see the heat radiating upward in dazzling waves, to see cotton blooming and the corn tasseling out. August was cotton-growing weather, and the hotter the better— cotton liked the blazing heat, chilled now and then by a short sudden August shower. The fields blossomed like islands in the South Seas, white and red splotches on a glorious green and crimson— the white and red hibiscus-like cotton flowers on the green cotton plants that spread away in long curving rows across the silky vermilion of the fields." Both writers note that this hot month of rest was reserved for the annual religious revivals at camp meetings. In the Strawberry Plains neighborhood, a large camp meeting was held at Wesley Campground, a six-acre tract lying in Section 26, Township 3, Range 3, on the northern bank of the Coldwater River. The Clopton tutor Seymour Carpenter remarks that it lasted for a week,

"The colored people held their services in a shed, about a hundred yards from the white people, " he tells us, "and I have never heard more moving music than their singing, especially at night, when, as they said, 'The power got hold of them.'"[6]

The August revival bolstered the faithful for the yearly routine of religious observances. We have already heard Carpenter's description of the slaves attending services at Wesley Chapel along with the Clopton family. Clara Clayton Fant's memoir of Wood-cote plantation adds more to our knowledge of slave religious life. Located ten miles to the northeast of Strawberry Plains, Wood-cote was a comparable land holding, supported by the labor of 140 blacks. Wood-cote slaves went twice a month to the master's church for a service just for them. Clara Fant notes their restrained, respectful attention to those sermons, and comments, like Carpenter, on the beauty and power of the singing: "Their whole hearts found utterance in the singing. They had remarkable voices, the men especially, and though altogether untaught, they sang with perfect time and harmony. As they neared the end of the hymns and their emotion increased, they would meet each other in the aisle, with a hearty and prolonged shaking of hands, but with no noise or confusion to disturb the music." In addition to these services at the white church, there were also religious observances at Wood-cote conducted by African American preachers on Sunday evenings, which were much more impassioned and emotional. The slave services mentioned in memoirs of Strawberry Plains were likely of the same order. Church was probably held in a shed or a barn or under a brush arbor that the slaves had constructed.[7]

After the time of rest and revival came fall, the season of unremitting labor from dawn to sundown. Throughout the workweek during the winter and the spring planting, workers assembled at the plantation kitchen for all meals, eaten either under large trees in fair weather or within doors around the huge fireplace. But during cotton-picking season, the midday meal was brought to the workers in the field, and all hands (men, women, and the older children) did not return for supper until dark. All year round, provisions were given to slave families for Sunday, when they cooked their own meals in their cabins.[8]

Early photograph of a Marshall County cotton field. Courtesy of the
Dean Collection, University of Mississippi

The end of the cotton harvest was celebrated with a barbeque. It
would have been, with seasonal culinary variations, like the annual
plantation barbeque given to celebrate the Fourth of July, when the
slaves at Wood-cote feasted on "whole Shoates and mutton," fresh
peaches, and early watermelon. Not long after the harvest celebration came Christmas, the "grand holiday of the year," the Wood-
cote mistress called it, and other observers confirm its importance
in the yearly cycle of slave life. The occasion was likely observed in
a similar fashion at Strawberry Plains: "Then there was no work for
four days, and dancing and feasting lasted through the whole. How
they did enjoy the dancing! The banjo and the fiddle were played as
fast as fast could be, but never too fast for the untiring feet, and the
'pigeon wing' was cut and the 'double shuffle' shuffled in a manner
wonderful to behold. At Christmas too were distributed new shoes,
hats, and clothes. There were great good boxes of them, and each
person was allowed to try on till suited. Then my father made a small
gift of money to them, giving most liberally to the hardest workers."
Here Mrs. Fant's account lends support to historians like Eugene
Genovese, who chronicle so well this enslaved race's amazing capacity
for both faith and joy under a repressive institution. It also puts in

context the old Strawberry Plains story that one year Eben Davis, as a special reward, presented his workers (perhaps only the "hardest workers") with top hats.[9]

Throughout the year, there were other special occasions, like the marriage between two slaves noted in Emma Finley's 1858 diary: "There is to be a wedding tonight—the happy couple James & Julia Ann; —the *wardrobe* almost completed, & cakes, pies, chickens, meats generally are in a state of preparation." Though denied the legal bonds of marriage by state law, slaves of the more religious masters and mistresses were sometimes joined in a ceremony performed on the steps of the big house, followed by a wedding feast. "I remember well when my nurse, whom I loved dearly, was married," Clara Clayton Fant wrote. "The bridal party came up to our house and stood in one of the porticoes; the bride dressed in a pretty white Swiss muslin, that fitted nicely her neat figure, with a single rose in her hair." At Wood-cote slaves were married by the family minister; whereas on the Finley and Davis plantations, the masters probably read the service. But at none of the three, apparently, were slaves married by the folk ceremony of jumping the broom stick.[10]

Simple recreations were enjoyed on Sundays and during lulls in the farming year. "De pleasures de slaves had," one former slave commented to a WPA interviewer, who was prone to broad dialectic transcriptions, "wuz things lak fishing, hunting, an' frolicing." Sundays and the slow periods in the agricultural cycle offered time for fishing and for hunting during the day or at night. Mrs. Fant ranks 'possom hunting as the male slaves' "chief amusement." She recalls, "On a bright moon light night the sounding of the horn and the barking of the dogs could be heard on the hills till far into the night." The "frolics," or dances, were so popular that when one was held on any plantation in the vicinity, neighboring planters would often provide passes so their slaves could go to them.[11]

Within the hierarchy of the plantation, a responsible, humane mistress contributed greatly to the health and welfare of the slaves. The eulogy of the "ole mistress," or "ole miss," of Wood-cote strikes the same notes sounded often in descriptions of the duties and skills of Martha Greenlee Davis: "It was she who visited and watched over the sick, saw they were well nursed and the doctor's directions followed. It was she who superintended the work of the women, the weaving, the spinning (for their clothes were made at home and the wheel and loom always going), the cutting out, the sewing, and the knitting, and saw that every man, woman, and child was well clothed." By all accounts, Martha Greenlee Davis filled conscientiously and ably the responsibilities of the mistress of a large plantation. The measure of respect felt for her is suggested by the loyalty of her servants during and after the war.[12]

Some others with whom the slaves were in close contact did not get such high marks. Former slaves expressed great bitterness toward the patrollers, who policed the neighborhoods trying to catch slaves who had left the home plantation without a pass. Stories of slaves eluding or escaping from them run throughout the area's WPA slave narratives. But the scorn evidenced for the patrollers was no match for the loathing expressed toward overseers. As one Marshall County slave voiced the feeling, the overseer "was death and gaul . . . common white trash." John Hebron Moore's history of antebellum Mississippi agriculture, *The Emergence of the Cotton Kingdom in the Old Southwest*, documents a decline in corporeal punishment by the mid-nineteenth century and finds that "progressive planters [instead] resorted to incentives during the later decades of the slavery era in an effort to obtain a maximum of labor from their slaves." But few, Moore acknowledges, "abandoned the use of the whip altogether," and whippings are reported in Seymour Carpenter's account of life on the Clopton plantation in 1846. Like the recruit, whose hostility is focused upon the drill sergeant rather than the company commander, slaves naturally hated most the overseer, the man who administered the lashes. Still, in the WPA narratives, former slaves were often candid in judging masters, as exemplified in the testimony of Jerry Howell of Marshall County, who judged his own master "mighty good," but the owner of the adjoining plantation "unmercifully cruel."[13]

The only surviving documentary evidence of Eben Davis's place on the scale of masters is the clause he wrote into the 1860 overseer's agreement requiring that Flippin "treat the slaves as humanely and kind as their conduct will allow." The clause, of course, is subject to various interpretations. But one thing certain is that, in the mid-1850s, the rhythm of labor changed at Strawberry Plains and the hard labor required of the strongest among the slave force increased.

In February 1855, Eben Davis reported to James Davidson in Virginia that there is "a great feeling manifested by the planters of the hill county to go to the bottom lands, for our hill county is exhausting so fast." Davis had purchased 10,000 acres in Arkansas for nineteen cents an acre, and in the fall of 1854, he had signed the first contract to construct part of the levee along the eastern bank of the Mississippi in exchange for land patents in the "Mississippi bottom," as the Delta was then called, the patents eventually totaling 30,000 acres. He cited as provocation that year's "poor crop which drove me into this speculation to give employment to my hands." Only male field hands were used for this heavy work, and after a few months Davis was asking Davidson's help in securing "some 6 or 8 negro men & boys."[14]

In early April 1856, he wrote Davidson that he had finished the levee, which he referred to with pride: "It is a grand piece of work." But he had met the terms of his contract only by keeping all his "efficient hands" at the river until the middle of March. Then bringing his work force back to Strawberry Plains, he had planted corn, but would not start planting cotton until late April.[15]

In the ensuing years he continued to counterbalance the demands of Strawberry Plains with his levee building, constantly moving slaves between the river and the Marshall County plantation. Two growing seasons later, in August 1858, Davis wrote that he was anticipating a record crop, while in the midst of another levee contract with "some 30 odd hands Leveeing on the Miss. river." He planned to bring them back to Strawberry Plains by October 1 to harvest the crop, and he commented, "Then nothing but Sickness, Sundays & rainydays will stop us."[16]

6

WAR

IN 1859 EBEN DAVIS doubled the size of his Marshall County acreage by purchasing the Roger Barton plantation immediately north of Strawberry Plains, which covered Section 1 and most of Section 36 and included half interest in a mill on the Coldwater River. By 1860 he also had title to thousands of acres in the Mississippi Delta counties of Sunflower, Tunica, Tallahatchie, Coahoma, Bolivar, and Washington, as well as tracts in Arkansas. The vast land holdings were a speculative venture. In a few years, Col. Davis, as he was now known, would be a man of great wealth—as long as the cotton economy remained strong.[1]

Toward the end of 1859, he had written his wife's nephew Greenlee Davidson expressing dismay over the actions of John Brown, that "disturber of the peace of mankind." Such dismay was only to increase with the growing sectional tensions over the next year. One measure of the gathering war clouds came in the fall of 1860, when St. Thomas Hall in Holly Springs, an Episcopal boys school considered one of Mississippi's best preparatory institutions, became a military school. Registered there with his cousin John Finley was Davis's oldest son, thirteen-year-old Eben Jr. The school received a signal honor in February 1861, when a group of senior cadets were chosen to accompany Jefferson Davis to Grand Junction, Tennessee, on his circuitous railroad journey to Montgomery to accept the presidency of the Confederate States of America.[2]

On March 28, 1861, answering President Davis's call for troops, three Marshall County volunteer companies left the Holly Springs depot, bound for Pensacola, Florida, to secure military installations on the Gulf. Three thousand citizens gathered to see them off amid

speeches and cheering. Within two weeks, Confederate troops fired
on Fort Sumter, and the war had begun. Ten days afterward another
company, the Confederate Guards, was formed in Holly Springs.
Among the volunteers were John Finley, then seventeen, and St.
Thomas Hall's commandant, Claudius Wistar Sears, born in Massa-
chusetts, educated at West Point, and ultimately awarded the rank of
brigadier general in the Confederate States Army.[3]

In late July, John Finley wrote his aunt at Strawberry Plains an ex-
cited letter describing the first major battle of the war, the Confederate victory at Bull Run. "We not only *whipped* them but completely
routed them," he boasted. He was safe, though "had my pants torn
by a bomb and also my shirt sleeve." Already, however, reports were
being received of Confederate deaths, one being that of the former
Davis overseer Booker Flippin.[4]

Still, life in northern Mississippi continued as far as possible in the
usual patterns. True, the iron foundry in Holly Springs had been converted to a small arms factory, and women met daily at the Masonic
Hall on the courthouse square to make clothes and bandages for the
soldiers. But cotton was planted and harvested, and some building
was even going on. The little school at Strawberry Plains was oper-
ating, and Eliza Jane Stephenson was riding over three times a week
to take music lessons from the Davis governess on the rosewood
piano in the front parlor. Col. Eben Davis was even engaged in marketing a new device of his invention:

Confederate Cotton Tie
E. N. Davis patented, Holly Springs, Miss.
Planters are invited to examine this new and valuable cotton tie,
which is the best and cheapest tie yet in use, and is destined to super-
cede both rope and iron, at less than half the costs.
    The bands for this tie can be made on the plantation by the ne-
gro at a season too when he can be best spared out of the field, from
the growth of timber anywhere suitable for hoops, such as hickory,
white or post oak xc.
    The simple and expeditious adjustment of this tie to the purpose
of baling cotton with *wooden* bands most providentially is discovered at this time, when other materials are almost denied the planter

and the Southern soil in all sections [illegible]. Orders solicited and
filled with dispatch.
  Address Eben N. Davis
  Holly Springs Miss.

By January 1862, more than ten thousand of the ties had been sold.[5]

All sense of normalcy ended, however, two months later as the
county made ready to receive casualties from the fighting in northeastern Mississippi. Both St. Thomas Hall and Holly Springs Female
Institute were commandeered for hospitals under the supervision
of local doctors, and early in April 1862 after the bloody battle of
Shiloh, the wounded filled not only the Holly Springs hospitals but
also makeshift infirmaries scattered from the town northward to
LaGrange, Tennessee. Among these were the Scales plantation house,
Oakland, at Scales (or Hudsonville) Depot on the Mississippi Central Railroad and the schoolhouse at Strawberry Plains five miles to
the southwest.[6]

War had come to what is today the Strawberry Plains Audubon
Center tract, and a soldier's unmarked grave in the Davis family cemetery bears silent witness. But we must now again broaden our canvas,
for the present tract covers three antebellum plantations that eventually came under the ownership of the Finley family. The Davis plantation, Strawberry Plains, is at the westernmost end. Adjoining it
on the east is the old McKissack place, and east of that, the Gibbons
plantation. Each has its own Civil War history.

John C. Gibbons had purchased a plantation of 640 acres in 1837
(Section 17, Township 3, Range 3) and added an additional 640 acres
in the 1840s (Section 8). By 1840, he was the owner of fifty-four
slaves and one of the wealthy planters of the county. The youngest
child of John C. Gibbons and his wife Jane Graves was a daughter,
Josephine, who was only thirteen when left an orphan by the death
of her father in 1853. Sent to boarding school at the Holly Springs Female Institute, she became a close friend of the Finley girls, and she
spent her holidays with her aunt, Nancy Graves Seal, wife of William
Seal, who in 1850 had bought the plantation bordering Strawberry
Plains on the south. In 1859 in the Seal home, the young heiress

Josephine Gibbons married William Anderson Roberts, and they set up housekeeping in the substantial Gibbons plantation house.[7]

Headwaters of the Coldwater River run through the Gibbons plantation. At the very northeastern edge is a site of recurring significance in the early history of Marshall County. Evidence suggests that it was here, in the elevated meadows along the southern banks of the river, that in the fall of 1837 the four thousand Chickasaws and their slaves were gathered before being moved to Memphis to cross the Mississippi. The site, which covered the northern reaches of Sections 8 and 9, most probably also later drew camp meetings like those described by the Clopton tutor in the 1840s. During the course of the Civil War, the Coldwater campground became a well-known destination point for both armies moving through the region. Its location, however, has presented problems to Civil War historians, first, because the term "Coldwater" used in dispatches and memoirs could mean any location on the meandering river, including the village of that name in the county to the west of Marshall. The problem was heightened in 1862, when commanders began to call Wall's station on the Mississippi Central Railroad west of the campground Coldwater Station.[8]

The first military force of record to occupy the campground was Col. William Hicks Jackson's Confederate cavalry, which struck repeatedly and effectively against the Union forces in Tennessee in the summer of 1862. Following the battle of Shiloh, Gen. William Tecumseh Sherman was sent to guard the railroad lines in western Tennessee and northwestern Mississippi. On June 27, 1862, Sherman wrote his sister that, since "the Enemy's Cavalry is as thick as thieves down about Coldwater, from which they can sally any night and rip up a few Rails," he had concluded that "we will have to go and attack them. We cannot tell how strong they are and must go it blind." Two days later, he ordered Gen. Stephen A. Hurlbut to leave behind detachments at Grand Junction and LaGrange, Tennessee, and move south toward Holly Springs. Sherman, likewise leaving some troops at Moscow, Tennessee, brought four thousand men to meet Hurlbut at Coldwater.[9]

The Confederates retreated before the superior force, and by nightfall several thousand Federal soldiers were spread over many acres surrounding the central camp. Sherman reported to Grant's head-

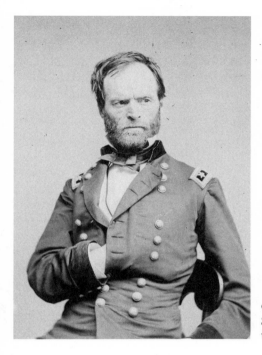

Gen. William Tecumseh
Sherman. Courtesy of
the Library of Congress

quarters, "I made my chief camp at Coldwater on account of water, which there [is] abundant, whilst at Holly Springs it is scarce." He commandeered rooms for himself and his aid-de-camp a mile distant in the Gibbons plantation house. The general had yet to earn his reputation for the mass destruction of total war, and Josephine Gibbons Roberts's descendants would recall Sherman without rancor, remembering that he "permitted no discourtesy to the family from his soldiers." He stationed a military guard at the house and issued daily supplies for both his own use and that of the family and servants, for whom separate meals were prepared.[10]

In July 1862, the *Memphis Daily Appeal* published a letter from Holly Springs reporting that Sherman's command had come "down to Cold Water [sic], on the road leading from this place to Lagrange [sic], and pitched their tents on the 29th ult" and over the next week had "overrun about half of our county." After successfully deploying troops as far south as the Tallahatchie River railroad bridge eighteen miles below Holly Springs, Sherman received orders on July 6 to return with his army to Tennessee. He wrote to his family rather bitterly two days later, "As long as I stay [at Coldwater] the Cavalry keeps back, but I was ordered back to the Line of Road and Jackson's Cavalry will be down on the Trains again."[11]

With Sherman's return to Tennessee, Marshall County was now back in Confederate control. In late July, Sherman was placed in command of Memphis, which Union troops had captured on June 6 and which they held for the rest of the war. Within a week, he was complaining to his family about the Confederate presence in Marshall County: "The Burning of cotton by the People of the South was one act of folly, but our buying the refuse of them for Gold & especially shipping salt, which from scarcity has risen to $100 a barrel, is a great act of folly. . . . If a Barrel of salt leaves town it is on its way to Holly Springs & the Secesh camp in half an hour." The Confederate government had ordered all Marshall County cotton burned in early June before the Sherman raid. But once the Union forces withdrew, some planter families found what unburnt cotton they could and ran it through the blockade to Memphis, where they exchanged it for needed supplies. Among the blockade runners were Martha Greenlee Davis of Strawberry Plains and her very independent and fearless nineteen-year-old neighbor Eliza Jane Stephenson. Each salvaged a bale from the charred remains on their plantations, put the cotton through a horse-driven gin, had the bales loaded on a wagon, and drove the wagon the fifty miles to Memphis. Cotton of course was contraband, and the two did not escape all censure, but several desperate grand ladies of Marshall were taking the same risk.[12]

In September 1862, the armies of Confederate generals Earl Van Dorn (known to his intimates as "Buck") and Sterling Price, estimated at more than fifteen thousand men, were brought from the trans-Mississippi theater and massed around Holly Springs and at Coldwater for deployment against the Federal Army in the northeastern corner of Mississippi. They met a staggering defeat at Corinth on October 5, and a week later they had fallen back to their old encampments. The entry of Gen. Van Dorn upon our scene in the fall of 1862 introduces one of the most fascinating interwoven threads of our narrative.[13]

"Van Dorn, with his light, graceful figure, florid face, light waving hair, and bright blue eyes," commented fellow officer Dabney Maury, "seemed made for love and war." The two-fold destiny would be his undoing, and that brings into our narrative the McKissack place, the third of the Audubon Center plantations. Lying between Strawberry Plains and the extensive Gibbons acreage, this plantation was purchased in 1854 by William McKissack, a wealthy investor of Spring Hill, Maury County, Tennessee. He died a year later without a will, and his entire estate was inherited equally by his six children, the youngest being a seventeen-year-old daughter, Jessie, who would lead Buck Van Dorn to his doom.[14]

Descended from the Peters family, a Tennessee dynasty quite as distinguished as the Perkins connection, Jessie McKissack was beautiful, strong willed, and tempestuous. Her pride of birth is reflected in a genealogical sketch she penned late in life. "My grandmother's name was Susan Peters," she wrote. "She married Colonel Jeffries of North Carolina, said to have been the wealthiest man in the State at the time—had a coach and four and outriders—my grandmother traveled in silk velvet." Jessie's general hauteur is given voice in a letter upbraiding a kinsman about a matter concerning her father's estate: "Well upon my word!! Ha! ha! seriously, Sir, you provoke a smile," she begins. She continues by invoking her reputation as a *"Tempest,"* and warns the man to *"weigh well* and *touch lightly* for your hand is in a *Lion's mouth."*[15]

In 1858 Jessie became the third wife of her cousin Dr. George Boddie Peters, twenty-six years her senior, and moved to his home in Bolivar, Tennessee. A member of St. James Episcopal Church in the village has recorded the parish's first glimpse of the new Mrs. Peters: "With plumes flying and silks rusting, Jessie swept into the church leaving the parishioners gasping. Her gown was elegant, her carriage regal, and her companion unbelievable. A black man trailed behind her and as she paused at the Peters pew, he quickly spread a large silk handkerchief on the seat. She settled herself gracefully and with some affection . . . as she knew all eyes were focused on her. The servant

handed her a small prayer book and left the church. Her entrance
never varied, but in time the routine became so commonplace it no
longer caused comment. She was always accompanied on her shop-
ping trips by a black servant and made a royal progress."

By the fall of 1862, she had borne George Boddie Peters two children. Through the intricate web of the Peters connection, she was
often drawn to Marshall County. The brother to whom she was closest, Alexander Cogle McKissack, a graduate of Yale, had bought out
the shares of his siblings in the Marshall County plantation, and he
and his wife had moved there in 1856. The fashionable couple were
immediately included in the highest social circles of the county and
the village of Holly Springs. During the war, Alex McKissack served
as colonel of a cavalry company that he had raised.[16]

Owning acreage near the McKissack land but living in town were
Dr. Peters's brother-in-law, wealthy planter William Arthur, and his
wife, the former Susan Peters. Their two daughters, called Pidge and
Beck, belles of their day, had married well—Pidge to a Peters cousin,
Thomas McNeill, a planter in the Mississippi Delta, and Beck to Confederate Gen. James R. Chalmers. Thus, the Peters-McKissack clan
was well represented in antebellum Marshall County. In the early
years of the twentieth century, old Holly Springs residents recalled
that other members of the McKissack family had "refugeed" (in local
parlance) to the town during the war. While there is no documentary
evidence that Jessie McKissack Peters, in particular, was at either the
McKissack plantation or in Holly Springs in the fall of 1862, in light
of subsequent events it seems likely that she was.[17]

Despite the Confederate losses, the fall of 1862 was the gayest period of the war for Marshall and Holly Springs. In October, schoolgirl Delia Scales of Oakland plantation, within three miles of the
Coldwater camp, gushed to her closest friend: "We have had the
house full of our soldiers ever since the *Yankees* left. I suppose you
know our army is encamped almost in sight of us. I was down at Gen.
Tillman's headquarters yesterday & had the pleasure of dining. . . . I
sent some wine down to them (the General and other officers there)
& I thought we would break up with a bran dance. Lou, I *do wish you*
were here, we would have *so much* fun." Fourteen years later and far

away in Boston, Holly Springs writer Sherwood Bonner would look back on this time: "Ah, those golden October days! Who among us can forget them? Houses were thrown open, and around every table gathered the gray-coated officers. Young girls taken from the school-room blossomed into belles and coquettes. Picnics, balls and reviews made every day 'run to golden sands.'"[18]

Col. William Hicks Jackson's cavalry again bivouacked at Cold-water, along with most of the rest of the army. Gen. Van Dorn, how-ever, had his headquarters and residence in the Magnolia Hotel, an elegant three-story structure on the Holly Springs square. He had returned after a staggering defeat and amid allegations of incompe-tence at Corinth, but to the military accusations were attached oth-ers: "There appears to be little in the way of factual support for the charges aimed at Van Dorn during the few weeks he spent at Holly Springs prior to and after the Battle of Corinth," his biographer comments, but he adds, "Unsubstantiated rumors, talk, and gos-sip were in ample supply, particularly after the remnants of the army reached Holly Springs." The same biographer quotes a Holly Springs citizen's letter to the Confederate Secretary of War stating, "General Van Dorn has sadly lost caste in this State by a course of life in pri-vate." Certainly the complaint was marital infidelity, and Sherwood Bonner suggests as much, noting that Holly Springs was a "strait-laced town, and Van Dorn was separated from his wife. Added to this, he had lost a recent battle, and the people were embittered against him. But his friends were devoted, and the officers of his staff loved him. . . . I know of no Southern officer who inspired such passionate attachment as the gallant and ill-fated Van Dorn. He seemed to live in an atmosphere of romance. When he showed his dark, haughty face in the ball-room not a girl among us would have refused him as a partner in spite of the warning looks of mammas and chaperons." One wonders whether it was in one of these ballrooms that Buck Van Dorn first encountered Jessie McKissack Peters and provided the ru-mors and gossip that were from that time attached to him.[19]

But early in November, any budding infatuation was ended abruptly—for the moment—with the news that the Union Army was moving south in force. In a dispatch headed "Mr. Roberts House,

One Mile from Coldwater, November 5, 1862—6:15 p. m.," Col. Jackson informed his commander Gen. Van Dorn that the Union Army had occupied Lamar eight miles to the north. He estimated the force at forty thousand.[20]

7

THE TWO ARMIES

ON NOVEMBER 3, 1862, a month after the fall of Corinth and just two days before news of the Union advance, a new commander, Gen. John C. Pemberton, reviewed the Confederate Army at Holly Springs. It was a grand occasion that drew many from the surrounding countryside, including Delia Scales of Oakland. "I felt so confident that our army intended making a stand," she wrote, "& that north Mississippi would be defended. But I soon found out it was a stampeed [sic] instead of a *stand* they anticipated making. Our souldiers [sic] were ready & *anxious* for a fight, & it was all owing to the *bad generalship* of Vandorn [sic] & Pemberton, that we did not drive the *last blue devil* from the country." Delia exaggerated the situation in several ways. This Marshall County campaign actually resembled more a chess game involving much maneuvering, advancing, and retreating. Writing from the village of Lamar to Gen. Ulysses S. Grant on November 8, a lieutenant was still unsure "whether the enemy are in strong force at Coldwater," just a few miles away. Col. Jackson's Rebel cavalry seemed to be everywhere, but the main body of the Confederate Army was in fact falling back in some disorder, though smaller pockets of troops remained behind. Finally, in a dispatch written at daybreak November 13 from Holly Springs, the commander of the 7th Kansas Cavalry could tell Grant: "I have just entered this city and my pickets are polluting the 'sacred soil' some 2 miles below it."[1]

Gen. Grant himself spent the last two days of November in the town before moving on to Oxford thirty miles to the south, where he established his headquarters. "As a handsome, pretty town," a correspondent for the *Chicago Times* reported, " too much cannot be said of Holly Springs; nor as a military position, too little. It is wholly untenable by any army, on account of the scarcity of water; possesses but few points of defense, and offers many of attack." This proved a prescient assessment. Grant, however, had decided to make Holly Springs his supply depot for the inland campaign against Vicksburg. Supplies of every sort made their way down the Mississippi Central Railroad to Holly Springs, and buildings both at the railway station and on the town square a mile away were filled with foodstuffs, clothing, supplies, and munitions. Grant's officers commandeered winter quarters in the houses of leading citizens, and Grant had even arranged that Mrs. Grant and their youngest child be housed in the grand Walter mansion.[2]

Troops were spread over the surrounding countryside—some forces at Lumpkin's Mill four miles south and others at Coldwater. Two of the soldiers encamped there commented on the natural environment. George Cadman told his wife, "this is a great country for persimmons and hickory nuts." Capt. Peter Casey of the Irish Legion, 90th Illinois Regiment, a saloonkeeper from Chicago, sent a fuller description. "It is very warm here, it is about as warm here in the winter as it is in Chicago in September. The woods is full of all kinds of birds and of all the colors of the rainbow. The woods look green as there is quite a number of trees here that grows all the year round such as holley the miselto and others and the grass and shrubs is all green. I sometimes forget it is winter."[3]

The men of the 90th Illinois arrived at Coldwater on December 6, and units were dispatched to guard various locations on the Mississippi Central Railroad. James Swan, the historian of the Irish Legion, locates their camp site as being "at the eastern edge of a much larger elevated area some two miles in extent that was known to, and alternatively occupied by, both Confederate and Union troops as 'Coldwater,' and variously reported as four to six miles north of Holly Springs." He also notes that "adjacent springs and small tributaries of the Coldwater River provided an abundant source of water, making the area a suitable camping area for large numbers of troops." The size of the camp is indicated by one of Capt. Casey's complaints to his wife about his duties as officer of the day: "Our lines take in 8 miles and the officer must keep on the move for 24 hours without any sleep and it is up and down hill and woods all the way. I can ride a

horse in daytime, but at night I have to go on foot." This was an initiation for the 90th Illinois, their first experience in the field, but, as
their quartermaster reported, the first weeks were relatively unevent-
ful. That was all to change on the morning of December 20, 1862.[4]

Shortly before sunrise, Gen. Earl Van Dorn's cavalry surprised
the Union garrison at Holly Springs, gained a surrender without a
fight, and burned over a million dollars worth of Federal munitions
and supplies. To prevent reinforcements, Van Dorn had posted Col.
William H. Jackson's troops between the town and the Union con-
tingent at Coldwater. The Coldwater camp was awakened at daylight by the sound of firing in the direction of Holly Springs followed shortly by the sight of smoke from the burning supplies. The
camp commander immediately ordered the regiment's white tents
taken down, so as not to reveal their numbers to the enemy. He then
aligned the troops on a hill in such a way that the force would appear larger than it was. About eleven o'clock, the Union troops first
engaged pickets of Jackson's cavalry, who continued to hover in the
vicinity for several hours, though never attempting to charge.[5]

By midafternoon, Van Dorn's force prepared to leave the chaotic
scene in Holly Springs. They had burned the former Rebel armory
(being used as a Union hospital), the roundhouse, and part of the
depot building, along with locomotives and railroad cars and three
bridges toward Coldwater. The Rebels had greedily equipped themselves, one later reporting that "every trooper had two to six pistols,
one or more carbines, one or more sabers, and all of the ammuni-
tion, rations, blankets, shirts, hats, boots, overcoats, etc, his horse
could carry." They had captured five hundred horses and mules, and
opened all Union and sutlers' supply stores to the citizenry, who were
carrying off great quantities of meat and grain. By Van Dorn's order
explosives were to be placed in small piles and detonated, but after
several hours of work, the three-story brick Masonic hall was still
half-full of materiel. Time was running out, and the hall was fired.
It is said that the building rose intact about 100 feet in the air and
then flew to pieces. The thunderous sound reverberated far past the
bounds of the Coldwater camp.[6]

This was Van Dorn's finest hour. Etched in the memory of a staff
member was the image of the general on his fine black mare, riding

The dashing and ill-fated Gen. Earl Van Dorn. Courtesy of the Mississippi Department of Archives and History

"straight as an Indian, sitting astride his horse like a knight, and looking every inch a soldier." His biographer calls the raid "the most spectacular victory" in the Mississippi theater that year. Shortly after four o'clock, Van Dorn's cavalry left Holly Springs, riding north, but they skirted Coldwater camp and proceeded parallel to the Mississippi Central, with parties sent out periodically to sever the telegraph lines and destroy sections of the road. While the Van Dorn raid may have been remembered locally as the "Glorious Twentieth," its aftermath was devastating.[7]

Amid conflicting reports of Van Dorn's whereabouts and his strength, the Union Army moved slowly to recapture Holly Springs. From Oxford, Grant dispatched an advanced guard, which reoccupied the town on December 21 and was joined two days later by the main body of the army. With his supply base decimated, Grant had decided to withdraw his forces to Memphis and assault Vicksburg by the river. Toward that end, he occupied Holly Springs as his headquarters from December 23 until January 10, 1863, while the railroad north to Grand Junction, Tennessee, was repaired. Because their food and forage had been destroyed by Van Dorn, Grant ordered his army to live off the countryside and sent heavily guarded wagon trains out to confiscated food and supplies from outlying plantations. From Holly Springs on January 4, he reported that "since the late raids this department, except troops on the river, have subsisted off the country. There will be but little in North Mississippi to support guerillas in a few weeks more."[8]

Strawberry Plains and other plantations near the Coldwater River felt the immediate effects of Grant's policy. Two days after the Van Dorn raid, a half mile from the Davis mansion, Maj. J. P. M. Stephenson was roused from his sickbed by the sound of the troops of Company C, 7th Kansas Jayhawkers, riding into the yard. He hastily dressed and ran from the house toward the barn and corn cribs, but his efforts to stop the soldiers were futile. An entry in one Jayhawker's diary records that they took "three loads of provisions, and several good horses and mules." Several years after the war, Stephenson descendants filed a claim against the government for compensation for stock, food, and forage:

> 9 head of horses at $150 (4 mules and 5 horses)
> 20 head cattle at $15
> 50 head hogs at $10
> 30 head of sheep at $3
> 3000 pounds of bacon at 15 cents
> 500 bushels of corn at 80 cents per bushel
> 2000 bundles of fodder at 3 cents
> 3 stacks of oats

The claim also notes that these Union raiders was followed by others.[9]

From exposure on that bitter, cold day, Maj. Stephenson developed pneumonia and died three weeks later. His neighbor Eben N. Davis was also marked by his first encounter with Union troops. When he remonstrated, perhaps fierily, with the foraging party that raided Strawberry Plains, a soldier savagely beat him with a rifle butt, leaving him bloody and dazed, as they plundered the plantation.[10]

When Eliza Jane Stephenson made her deposition in support of the Davis claim for war losses, it was forty years after the fact, and she was of necessity vague. "Mr. Davis bought provisions by the

wholesale, had large family & negroes by the hundreds," she testi-
fied. "So he had mules & horses & cows, calves, sheep & quantities
of provender—all of which was taken by Grant's Army. The farm was
right at their camp." The 1860 agricultural census shows that the resources of Strawberry Plains, which were indeed bountiful, included
4 horses, 26 asses and mules, 10 milch cows, 18 working oxen, 17
other cattle, 60 sheep, 200 swine, 1000 bushels of wheat, and 10,000
bushels of Indian corn. Previously the ample stores of the plantation
had furnished supplies to various neighbors and friends. Just a few
months before, Mrs. Alexander McKissack had sent a note apologiz-
ing for forgetting to pay for twenty-five pounds of flour, a bushel of
sweet potatoes, spare ribs, and a kid that Mrs. Davis sent "when I expected Mrs. Smith & Mrs. James Anderson to dine with me." Now
Strawberry Plains could barely sustain its own, and there would be
no further elegant social occasions for anyone in the neighborhood,
including the fashionable McKissacks.[11]

By January 10, 1863, all of Grant's army had withdrawn from Holly
Springs. Anxious to prevent incendiaries from firing the city in re-
taliation for the Van Dorn raid, Gen. Grant charged his junior officers to keep strict control over the troops. After the evacuation,
Gen. James B. McPherson reported to Grant that he had been successful in preventing burning, except in the case of some small, unoccupied structures and the Magnolia Hotel, which had housed so
sumptuously men of both armies. But a druggist writing to an absent
townsman gave a far different report of "the Fiends in blue garb."
"My losses are fearful," he said. "My residence robbed of every dollar's worth of provisions and every room sacked and pillaged. I have
no physic left. All the Drug Stores totally destroyed, Dr. Dougherty
and Dr. Caruther's offices also demolished." Twelve residences had
been consumed, several business houses on the square, a tan yard,
a steam mill, a gin makers shop, a carpenters shop, the jug factory,
five stables, and the town gas plant. Numerous other buildings, including the Episcopal church, had been fired but extinguished. So
dramatic were the conflagrations that a reporter attached to the 12th
Wisconsin told his paper, "We left Holly Springs about dark on the
evening of the 10th, and marched to Cold Water [sic] some five miles
distant. There was no moon, but from the light of the burning city,

we could plainly see our way nearly the whole distance." By the next day all of the troops had reached Tennessee. From Holly Springs on January 16, Mildred Strickland wrote her husband, "I don't think the Yanks will be here any more. There is nothing to come for now."[12]

Another phase of the war had ended for Marshall County, but the story of Buck Van Dorn and Jessie McKissack Peters continued. After the Holly Springs raid, Van Dorn's cavalry made a foray into western Tennessee before sweeping back to their headquarters in Grenada, Mississippi. Then Van Dorn did a surprising thing—he took a brief furlough in early January to visit his wife and children, whom he had not seen in over two years. Apparently any marital discord was put behind them, and the couple reconciled before he received orders to join forces with Nathan Bedford Forrest in Tennessee. Union troops occupied both Memphis and Nashville, and Van Dorn and Forrest were assigned to keep these two armies separated. Was it fate, chance, or careful planning that placed Van Dorn's headquarters that March in Spring Hill, Maury County, Tennessee, where Jessie McKissack Peters was then living on a plantation inherited from her father, while her husband was away attending to his land holdings in Arkansas?[13]

For Van Dorn's first weeks in Tennessee, he and Forrest were almost constantly in their saddles, skirmishing with the enemy at various points in Middle Tennessee. By the end of March, they had succeeded in blocking any serious Union advance from Nashville to the south and west, and Van Dorn's horsemen could now settle into the kind of daily military routine and active social life that they had enjoyed in Holly Springs the previous fall. Amid the balls and reviews, there were still tensions. At one point, Van Dorn and Forrest argued so vehemently that a duel was only narrowly averted. Van Dorn's blood still could run hot.[14]

From the time of his arrival in Spring Hill, Van Dorn and Jessie McKissack Peters had been the subject of gossip. When Jessie first appeared at the general's headquarters in the Aaron White mansion, Mrs. White had asked her to be seated in the parlor while she told the general of Mrs. Peters's presence. Sweeping past her startled hostess and ascending the stairs, Jessie set out unannounced to find Van Dorn, and they remained closeted for an hour. A few days later, Mrs. Peters, handsomely dressed in a black riding habit topped by a stylish hat with an ostrich feather, again rode up to the White residence, tossed the reins to the general's orderly, and summarily entered. Mrs. White refused to countenance this impropriety and brought pressure upon her husband to ask the general to change his residence. After Van Dorn had moved to another brick mansion in the village, he and Jessie were frequently seen taking afternoon drives in her fine carriage.[15]

Dr. George Peters returned to Spring Hill from his Arkansas plantation on April 12. According to a deposition he later gave, he was met immediately by the gossip about Van Dorn and his wife. Gen. Van Dorn's adjutant, Maj. Manning M. Kimmel, recalled that about April 27 Jessie McKissack Peters offered a cabin on her plantation to the general so he could be near the bivouac of his troops. Shortly after the general moved in, she invited him and his staff to a dance in the plantation house, which occasioned a heated argument between the doctor and his wife that Kimmel overheard. Within a day or two, the adjutant approached Van Dorn. "General, as your friend," he began, "may I take the liberty of warning you that your friend, Mrs. Peters, can cause you a lot of trouble." Buck Van Dorn denied any intimacy and spurned the advice: "I have no intention of getting involved with her. However, I find her to be pleasant company. She is undoubtedly the smartest woman I have ever known. She is well informed on many subjects, and a most interesting conversationalist. Headstrong and willful, yes, but very charming and mysterious. She intrigues me. In many ways, she has great talent. In running her plantation, practically alone, she shows much executive ability, not ordinarily found in a woman. Besides, she is a very patriotic lady to so willingly allow our troops to mess up her beautiful plantation. You and I are enjoying her hospitality, and some of her best whiskey, which she has so kindly given to us to help us forget the horrors of war."[16]

Subsequently, after Dr. Peters had been away from the plantation on a trip to Nashville, he learned that Van Dorn had visited Jessie every night during his absence. According to his deposition, he then set a trap. In early May, he pretended to leave once again, but "on the second night after my supposed and pretended absence, I came upon the creature, about half past two o'clock in the morning, where I expected to find him." Shortly before nine o'clock on the morning of May 7, Dr. Peters entered Van Dorn's headquarters in Spring Hill. The general was sitting at his desk with his back to the door. Peters fired his pistol, lodged a bullet in the back of the Van Dorn's skull, and rode hard toward the Union garrison at Nashville. The hero of Holly Springs was dead, but Jessie McKissack Peters was to live for sixty more years and to be involved again, decades later, in the history of the McKissack plantation on the Audubon Center tract.[17]

8

DEVASTATION

U LYSSES S. GRANT wrote in his *Memoirs* that shortly before
he withdrew his troops from Marshall County on January 10,
1863, the local people asked him how they were to survive in this now
despoiled country. He recalled that he "advised them to emigrate."
Living conditions were desperate. To increase the sense of desola-
tion, within a few days the region had the deepest snowfall within
memory.[1]

Writing to a friend, a Holly Springs townsman painted a grim
picture of the outlying plantations, plundered by the blue-coated
army and now deserted by great numbers of the slave workers: "In
the country all is gone, corn, fodder, meat, flour, all their provisions,
all their stock, wagons, teams, vehicles of every description—Fences
and Negroes. I heard a gentleman say a few days since that not less
than ten thousand negroes were congregated around the Junction
& LaGrange. I do not think this an exaggeration, but far under the
number. I know of a number of men in the county who have lost
from 25 to 100 of them." The slaves had left in a desperate and, for
most of them, a doomed march toward freedom. Lincoln had issued
the Emancipation Proclamation on September 22, 1862, to take effect
on the first day of 1863. As the Union armies moved into the Deep
South, word was spread among the slaves, and by November 1862
they were fleeing plantations and following the Federal troops. On
November 15, Grant wrote from LaGrange to Gen. Henry W. Halleck
at the War Department, "Negroes [are] coming in by wagon loads.
What will I do with them?" Halleck replied: "The Secretary of War
directs that you employ the refugee negroes as teamsters, laborers, xc,
so far as you have use for them, in the quartermaster's department on
forts, railroads, xc; also in picking and removing cotton, on account

of the Government. So far as possible subsist them and your army on the rebel inhabitants of Mississippi." Grant's solution was to set up a huge camp for the fugitive slaves at Grand Junction, Tennessee, under the command of Chaplain John Eaton of the 27th Ohio. "With such an army of them, of all ages and both sexes, as had congregated about Grand Junction, amounting to many thousands, it was impossible to advance," Grant wrote in his *Memoirs*. "There was no special authority for feeding them unless they were employed as teamsters, cooks, and pioneers with the army, but only able-bodied young men were suited for such work. This labor would support but a very limited percentage of them."[2]

Grant had been given a tremendous responsibility without the necessary resources to fulfill it. In his 1907 book, *Grant, Lincoln, and the Freedmen*, John Eaton cites the following account of a subordinate that conveys a sense of the tragic situation at Grand Junction: "I hope I may never be called on again to witness the horrible scenes I saw in those first days of the history of the freedmen in the Mississippi Valley. Assistants were hard to get, especially the kind that would do any good in our camps. A detailed soldier in each camp of a thousand people was the best that could be done. His duties were so onerous that he ended by doing nothing. . . . In reviewing the condition of the people at the time, I am not surprised at the marvelous stories told by visitors who caught an occasional glimpse of the misery and wretchedness in these camps." Eaton's camp was recognized as the beginning of the Freedmen's Bureau, the agency formed to oversee the welfare of the freed slaves, but the immediate issue of what to do with the refugees was complicated for many months by differences in policy between the civil government and the military—and most desperately by the miserable conditions within the camp itself. After leaving the Coldwater camp on December 27, 1862, Union soldier George Cadman wrote home cynically, "While there numbers of niggers passed, all going norf, as they called it. Poor fools. They will be worse off in a year's time than they are now."[3]

The columns of slaves moving northward dramatically increased with the news that Grant was abandoning northern Mississippi. As the troops withdrew from Holly Springs, there was a chaotic clambering upon the railroad cars leaving the Mississippi Central depot.

Mildred Strickland reported to her husband that all her slaves slipped off that night after supper and escaped on the last train. Planter Robert Burrell Alexander of Happy Hill plantation a mile south of town, who in 1860 owned eighty-five slaves, made this entry in his diary: "71 negroes went to the Yanks have 3 old men & a few women and children left." The exodus from Happy Hill was typical of plantations in central Marshall County.[4]

Alexander follows that entry by noting, "Wife left at ten o'clock today to go to Lagrange Tenn for mules, to try to get a wagon and team." The exigencies of war were bringing out the mettle of Southern women. Rebel families also had to eat. The Greenlee women not unexpectedly rose to the demands of the times. Taking her oldest son with her on mounts she had borrowed, Martha Davis also made the trip to the Federal garrison at LaGrange, where she persisted until she had seen the commanding officer, who agreed to release some of her confiscated stock.[5]

In January 1863, Grant had the freedmen's camp moved to Memphis, where an ironic practice was continued despite Lincoln's proclamation. As had been the policy of many Union commanders almost since the beginning of the war, "slave hunters" were permitted to visit the encampments. The Alexander diary reveals that in mid-February the master of Happy Hill secured the services of one of these hunters, and the Strickland letters document that a number of owners themselves went to Memphis to find their slaves. Writing just two weeks earlier, a Kansas Jayhawker blamed Gen. Halleck for continuing the practice "that all slaves within any camp should be delivered to the owners if the owner should come for them." So in the midst of this war fought in part over the issue of slavery, Marshall County slave owners were allowed to retrieve their slaves. "How much are you willing to pay for Hardin?" Mildred Strickland asked her husband. "Perhaps I could hire a man to get her out of the lines." On March 19, she reported that Mary Jane Finley had returned from Memphis with eight of her slaves. Eleven days later, Robert Alexander made this diary entry: "I saw Mrs. Finley on the street & she said she was going back to Memphis after the Ballance [sic] of her negroes. She had 28 left, 8 died, [had already] brot home 8." The deplorable conditions of the camps and the frequent deaths were now bitter realities confronting those seeking their freedom. Another Strickland letter reveals that in Memphis the former slaves had to express their wish to leave the camp. Mrs. Strickland tells her husband that she will find her slaves there and "see whether they want to come home." In the midst of these confused policies, further confusion was added within the camps by the War Department decision to make soldiers of the former slaves. The perceived threat of conscription seems to have tipped the balance to make the male freedmen decide to leave the dismal camps and return to their home plantations.[6]

By late spring, with most of his slaves now returned, Col. Eben Davis decided to remove most of the field workers to Alabama to make a crop. Clearly, Marshall County would remain contested territory between the two armies, and the Confederacy needed cotton revenue to finance the war. Two neighboring planters, John M. Anderson and William Seal, had moved their slaves to Texas before the Grant invasion, and Martha Greenlee Davis had been urging her husband to leave Strawberry Plains since he was beaten after the Van Dorn raid. Now with the added incentive of keeping his reduced slave force out of the way of Yankee armies, he made the decision. His Marshall County tax receipt for 1863 and 1864 charges him with only twenty slaves in the county. His wife, with atavistic strength of purpose, remained at Strawberry Plains with this group of slaves to guard her home.[7]

At the end of the summer of 1863 during the lull between cultivation and the season for harvesting, Col. Davis was back in Marshall County, as was his nephew George Finley, who had been wounded in the Confederate service. A year earlier, George and his younger brother John (whose first term of enlistment had expired) had joined a company that Capt. Thomas Webber was raising for John Hunt Morgan's celebrated 2nd Kentucky Cavalry. The unit, Company F, was filled with Marshall Countians, one of the fiercest being their cousin Sam Finley, who enlisted when he was not yet fifteen. At Woodland on furlough after being wounded, George was hurriedly attending to as much family business as he could. One concern was the Finley slaves in Alabama. They had been hired out to the Rebel armory in Holly Springs. In advance of Grant's army, the owners,

Jones and McElwain, had moved the armory to Birmingham. George Finley sent this note by his uncle to two of his slaves:

> To Tom & Edmund
> I have heard that you were not well fed and clothed by Mr. McElwain as he promised me he would. And as Uncle Davis is going over to see after his people I have gotten him to attend to you also. He may think it advisable to move you from the Iron Works. If so it will only be nearby somewhere where you will be better cared for and in the country on farms. He will in that case have to separate you but will keep the families together. Becky wishes Wash to take Ike with him if you go. I have been wounded and have been at home a short time but will leave again day after tomorrow. All are very well at home and doing well considering the number of times the Yankees have come down. They are taking all the negro men they can catch to put in their army. We have heard that Bob & [illegible] are dead but don't know whether it is so or not. Dr. Moseley says a great many are coming home in his neighborhood. Dr. Dunlap is going to take Charlotte over to Ala. to his other folks next week. One of the girls will write to me of you when Uncle Davis goes over as I won't be here then.
> Good Bye
> George J. Finley

The letter not only reveals the expected Finley consideration and tone, but also confirms the fact that others at the time still considered Alabama a safe haven. The schoolgirl Sherwood Bonner, in fact, was sent to a boarding school in Montgomery following the Van Dorn raid.[8]

The Marshall County countryside was anything but a haven. The Alexander Civil War diary bears witness to the continued uncertainties of living under the threat of invasion, with the only hope of protection from the Union troops being the Confederate cavalry company of Capt. Billy Mitchell, raised in the Coldwater countryside and active locally through much of the conflict. The constant menace the citizens faced was even voiced in a local song, "The Yankees Are Coming," sung to the tune of "The Campbells are Coming."

Nine of its ten stanzas were preserved in the ledger of a country store a few miles west of Strawberry Plains:

The Yankees are coming! Away! Which Way?
Who saw them? Do tell us. And what did they?
Are they infantry, cavalry? How many? How far?
Fifteen hundred, they say and are at Lamar.

The Yankees are coming! They'll be here by daylight,
Until the brave Mitchell shall put them to flight,
Or ambush and whip them, as often he has done,
With his handful of men and the double-barrel'd gun.

The Yankees are coming! Did you hear that drum?
Hark! Boom goes the cannon! They surely do come,
With Matches! They'll steal the last mule that we have,
For thieves they are all, up to Grant and his staff.

The Yankees are coming! Send the news round and round,
They're many, says a courier, but three miles from town.
Oh mercy! they are here. You may run if you will,
But yonder they rise o'er the top of a hill.

The Yankees are coming! See, they dash through the street.
Some are looking for mules, and others for meat.
Bang. Down goes the door, and out go the mules
With saddles and harness and all sorts of tools.

The Yankees are come, vile thieves that they are.
Thus are old men and women to wage such a war.
They spoil all our gardens; not a chicken they spare,
To an old sitting hen and the clothes your babes wear.

The Yankees are come! Yes, alas it is true,
Each one of them breeched in his sky blue.
I hear their sabers. Clatter, clatter! they go.
How fiendish they look. They're jayhawkers, I know.

Now Yankees are come—yes, the worst of the crew,
From Iowa, Kansas, and Illinois too.

To restore the blest Union at Abraham's call,
The negroes set free and drive Secesh to the wall.

The Yankees are come! How madly they rave!
The rebellion they'll crush and Vicksburg they'll have.
In their efforts they say they will never relax
Till Pemberton's whipped, or they die in their tracks.

On one of columns in the colonnade of the Hugh Craft house in
Holly Springs, a family member kept a record of fifty Union raids on
the town. The Coldwater camp was occupied time and time again
for short periods, and Strawberry Plains frequently felt the effects.
Martha Greenlee Davis managed as best she could, hiding stock and
food from the foraging parties, and running the Memphis blockade with Eliza Jane Stephenson to replenish lost supplies. The Yankee
soldiers took to calling Mrs. Davis "Old Secesh," an epithet that she
hated, and to taunting her with comparisons to a goose, "Well, we
pick you clean every time we come, and the next time you're all feath-
ered up again." She was particularly angered by the party that ran-
sacked her wardrobe and carried their plunder off in saddlebags im-
provised from her bloomers slung over their horses.[9]

Martha did find devious ways to revenge herself against the invaders. After one raiding party dumped a hogshead of flour on the
ground and then stomped and spat to render it unusable, she directed
children and servants to scrape the befouled mass back into the bar-
rel for the next party to find. Everyone on the place also had an assigned duty whenever the Yankees were suspected in the neighborhood. Young Johnny Davis would speak in old age of the best meal
he had ever eaten—one that Mrs. Stephenson sent to him in a tin cup
when he was hiding a cow from the Yankees.[10]

By the winter of 1863–1864, the situation was grim. One wounded
Confederate soldier wrote from Holly Spring on December 6: "This
country still continues to be contested ground—one day Yank, one
day Reb. . . . You can imagine I have no pleasant time hiding today,
out tomorrow. We are almost eat out of house—and living is getting
to be a matter of thought and anxiety. But I hope we will get through

without starving." A boy in the area, John Mickle, would remember, "People resorted to crude methods for a food supply. Roasting ears were grated on large tin graters, like nutmeg graters, and used for bread. Toasted dried corn was ground and used for coffee, and tea was made from sassafras leaves. Most families kept a cow and had milk and butter. . . . People ate meat when they could get it." In fact, it was the question of meat that finally sealed the fate of Strawberry Plains.[11]

Taking advantage of the military confusion at the end of 1863, the Davis retainers had slaughtered some of the hogs hidden in the woods and put the meat in the smoke house to season. But the Yankees were soon again dispatched to the region. On January 11, 1864, Gen. Benjamin Grierson, now Federal commander at Memphis, sent this message to Lt. Belden, Adjutant of the 6th Illinois Cavalry: "The rebels are reported bridging Coldwater at Lockhart's Mill and half mile below at Rhoads' farm, and at some point between Lockhart's Mill and Hudsonville. You will send patrols to all points on Coldwater west of Lockhart's Mill and obtain all possible information of the movements of the enemy." Lockhart's Mill (in which Eben Davis had purchased half interest in 1859) and the Rhodes place on the Coldwater River lay only two miles north of Strawberry Plains on Mt. Pleasant Road, and one of these patrols may well have been the Union unit that appeared at the plantation so quietly on a January day that their presence was a total surprise. Seeing the soldiers enter the smoke house, Mrs. Davis left the mansion with a pistol hidden under her apron in the folds of her dress, as was now her custom. Confronting the men carrying out the meat, she begged them to leave something for her children. They laughed, and a rough-looking, wild-eyed soldier cursed her. When she protested such behavior, he repeated the curse and follow it by taunting, "Now, damn you, what can you possibly do against all of us?" Frightened and trembling, she drew the pistol from beneath the apron and shot him in the head.[12]

At first stunned as they watched their comrade fall, the soldiers then rushed the shaken woman to wrest the smoking gun from her grasp. At the same moment, the sound of the shot drew an officer to the scene. He stopped the struggle and took the pistol. After questioning the party, he pronounced Mrs. Davis's action justified and ordered the men to leave and bury their dead. She had escaped penalty for the moment.

But a few months later the last Union raiding party that Strawberry Plains was to see rode up. Pounding the double doors with his rifle stock, the soldier in charge ordered the family from the house. The Yankees were going to burn it; penalty had only been delayed. Martha Davis pled for more time because her eldest son, Eb, was seriously ill, and should not be moved. The officer was adamant; she had fifteen minutes to remove the family and salvage anything she might. Some of the men offered to carry the feverish boy out of the house, but he snapped at them that he would crawl out first. Others, however, began assisting the family and servants in saving what they could—clothing, papers, some of the parlor furniture. At the end of the quarter hour, an order was given to chop into kindling the piano, which had been being dragged as far as the hall. The tinder was then scattered through the house and ignited. The fire roared upward. In less than an hour only the charred walls were left standing.[13]

Mrs. Davis now had to force herself out of her shock. There was no time to indulge her outrage; she had to take matters in hand. She decided quickly that she would not leave Strawberry Plains. She sent the children to her sister at Woodland, except for her oldest son and her youngest daughter, Augusta, who was only four. They slept that night across the ravine in the servants' quarters, where they lived for the rest of the war. With the aid of her small corps of loyal servants, she kept the farm running.

In the midst of wartime deprivation, the petted, spoiled Mildred Thomson Strickland of Holly Springs, product of a Philadelphia finishing school, complained to her husband, "I shall have to throw every accomplishment aside and go to the wash tub." Martha Greenlee Davis uttered no complaints, then or later. She simply did what she had to do, and the privileged Rockbridge belle learned all sorts of skills never before required of her. Among the remaining servants, the most supportive were Frank and Margaret Lee, near neighbors now in the quarters. Under the tutelage of Aunt Margaret, Mrs. Davis had become an excellent cook by the end of the war. Many a time she had also gone to the wash tub.[14]

When the long war was finally over, despite the series of battles lost, many people in the countryside did not wish to believe the news of Appomattox and accept the defeat of the hopes that had sustained them. That spring of 1865, Col. Eben Davis returned from Alabama. He was sixty-three years old and crippled in one leg from osteomyelitis. The ruins of the plantation house looming up must have seemed a symbol of the South's devastation.[15]

9

HARD TIMES

A NORTHERN JOURNALIST touring the South in the year after the war wrote of an evening spent on the Mississippi Central Railroad riding up through Marshall County toward Grand Junction as "a dismal night of thumpings over broken rails, and lurches and contortions of the cars, as if we were really trying in our motion to imitate the course of the rails the Yankee raiders had twisted." Had he traveled by day, he would have seen other evidences of the war upon this landscape. Almost all of the fencing was gone, burned by one or another of the occupying armies. The stock was depleted by the many raids, and the neglected land was beginning to erode. Hard times were upon the land, and it would be decades before the picture brightened.[1]

Before Col. Eben Davis could attend to any of the many material concerns involving his plantation, there was a family matter that required immediate attention. His oldest son, Eben Jr., had spent a difficult adolescence at Strawberry Plains during the war. For the last year, he had lived in the slave quarters with only his mother and small sister for company. Fiery, moody, and very lonely, the seventeen-year-old Eben formed an attachment with a slave girl of his age, Susan, on the Stephenson plantation just half a mile away. On September 30, 1865, she gave birth to his child, whose name was recorded in the Stephenson slave register as Zeek. He would always bear his mother's surname.[2]

The 1860 census reported that thirteen percent of the slave population in the South was "mulatto," the blanket term used for all with white ancestry. While that figure alone does not support the "harems of abolitionist fantasy," it does reflect the long history of interracial mixing. "The intimacy of the Big House and of the paternalistic master-slave relationship in general," Genovese writes, "manifested itself as acts of love in the best cases, sadistic violence in the worst, and ostensible seduction and imposed lust in the typical." The only descendants of this particular union to comment upon it suggest that "there was love in it." That view may be borne out by events in 1865. According to Col. Davis's granddaughter, in the fall of 1865 he took his son to Tuscaloosa and enrolled him at the University of Alabama, but Eben Jr. "beat him back home."[3]

Young Eben appears to have been the most difficult of the children, a loner, the least agreeable, and the most remote. From our vantage point, he is simply opaque. He and Susan Stephenson could have found in each other the sustaining affection that each needed, and their relationship may have lasted after Zeek's birth. Some of Zeek's descendants suggest that it continued even after the marriage of Susan to a black man in 1867 and that her husband's jealousy and subsequent abuse over her relationship with Davis contributed to her death in the early 1870s during a pregnancy. Evidence and accounts are contradictory. We shall probably never know. But Eben Jr. and his son Zeek Stephenson continued to live in proximity all their lives— a situation filled with many ironies.[4]

Men in the neighborhood knew Zeek's parentage, and the manager of the Stephenson plantation even wickedly took pleasure in giving the 1880 census taker Zeek's name as "Zeek Davis." As was often the case, it appears that the knowledge of his paternity was kept from the women on both plantations. Apparently Eben's mother was not aware of his having fathered the child, and I believe that his niece never knew. After Eben's return from Alabama, Col. Davis arranged a job for his son working on the Mississippi levees, which kept him away from Strawberry Plains a good part of the year.

Col. Eben Davis found himself now "land poor." With title to thousands of acres, he had not the means to pay the taxes. He would have to borrow against his future crops and his land holdings. When the war ended in April 1865 the planting season was far advanced, so no one expected more than a meager yield. Many looked upon 1866 as the test. In early March of that year, Col. Davis mortgaged the original Strawberry Plains plantation consisting of Section 12 and the northern half of Section 7 in an attempt to hold off his creditors and finance a real crop again. On May 4, the Holly Springs *Reporter* commented that "the cotton is up generally with as good or better stand than usual. . . . If the seasons are favorable and the freedmen work faithfully for the next three months, we may expect Marshall county to raise twelve to fifteen thousand bales, about one fourth of the average crop." The leadership were summoning all the optimism that they could.[5]

In the midst of cautious hope for the future, former Confederates were also determined to memorialize their recent past. In April 1866, the ladies of Holly Springs gathered at the town cemetery in late afternoon with wreaths of flowers to place on the graves of fallen soldiers. Already a group of townsmen had laid plans to erect a monument to fallen comrades. Toward that end, they were planning an equestrian tournament in midsummer to raise funds. These contests of daring and skill in which horsemen riding at full gallop attempted to collect upon their long lances a series of rings (suspended from poles) harkened back to the middle ages. The Romantic interest in medievalism brought a revival of interest in the sport in the nineteenth-century South, where such events enjoyed enormous popularity. In *A Distant Mirror: The Calamitous 14th Century*, historian Barbara Tuchman provides a rich description of the prototype: "With brilliantly dressed spectators in the stands, flags and ribbons fluttering, the music of trumpets, the parade of combatants making their draped horses prance and champ on golden bridles, the glitter of harness and shields, the throwing of ladies' scarves and sleeves to their favorites, the bow of the heralds to the presiding prince who proclaimed the rules, the cry of poursuivants announcing their champions, the tournament was the peak of nobility's pride and delight in its own valor and beauty." Such a scene transposed to Mississippi seemed the perfect enactment of the Southern chivalric ideal.[6]

The closest jousting field to Strawberry Plains lay only just over the western hedgerow on the Stephenson plantation. By July young men of the neighborhood and beyond, like the Finleys, had been practicing there for weeks, and a series of jousts had narrowed the field of contestants. Newspapers throughout the region carried notices of the impending Grand Tournament in Holly Springs, and the presidents of both the Mississippi Central and the Memphis and Charleston Railroads offered half fares to those traveling to the event, which was to end the first night with a concert and *tableaux vivante* and was to be concluded the second night with a ball.[7]

On July 18, the two-day tournament opened at Powell's Grove on the outskirts of Holly Springs. The first prize was announced as a diamond ring, the second, a fine saddle, the third, a silver cup. It was the first great public social event in the region since the war, and an estimated crowd of nearly five thousand people flocked to the field. At the end of the second day, the Knight of Douglas, who lived a hundred miles distant, was declared winner, with eleven rings garnered in three tiltings. He chose a Methodist minister's daughter Queen of Love and Beauty. Those who had trained near Strawberry Plains were well represented. The Knight of Twelfth Night or What You Will, who came in second with ten rings, was Martha Greenlee Davis's nephew young John S. Finley, lately of Gen. John Hunt Morgan's cavalry. Competing in the separate Horsemanship Contest, along with several older veterans of Morgan's troupe, was the sixteen-year-old schoolboy Lea Stephenson.[8]

During the two days, the Monument Association raised more than twenty-five hundred dollars from the tournament. But the enthusiastically collected funds fell victim to the times. Ill-advisedly loaned out, they were never paid back—a mark of the economic instability of the period. In fact by the time the tournament took place, grim signs were already darkening the immediate future. After taking the Mississippi Central to Holly Springs, the correspondent for a Memphis newspaper wrote back, "farmers have done what they could with their limited means since the war, but the country all along the road is still a wreck of former prosperity." The cotton crop, about which local leaders had expressed optimism a few months previously, the correspondent judged "barely middling in prospect." By fall Marshall County planters, among them Col. Eben Davis, had realized that they must pin their hopes on the 1867 crop.[9]

The Davis parents and their five children were still living in the servants' quarters, and at the beginning of 1867 Col. Davis went even deeper in debt in order to make the mansion house at Strawberry Plains habitable again. By April, work was progressing on the charred shell. In relation to the former grandeur of the structure, the rebuilding efforts were modest. All windows and most doors were re-placed, but neither the front nor back porticos were rebuilt. The hall was left with bare brick walls, along one of which ran a crude set of steps to the second floor. Only the two rooms to the east of the hall on both floors were plastered and finished. The front room on the east became the parlor, furnished with a carpet, a hanging lamp, and the furniture saved from the fire. This patched-together structure would house the Davises for another hundred years.[10]

A year earlier the Holly Springs *Reporter* had issued a plea for the forbearance to the creditors of local planters until they could get on their feet again: "In Marshall county [sic], in the March term of the Circuit Court, *five hundred and eighteen* suits were brought involv-ing an immense amount of money, and where it is to come from we are at a loss to tell, as hundreds of those who have been sued have not made a dollar clear of expenses since 1861. The people of Marshall wish to pay their debts, and will use every exertion in their power to do so, but if executions are issued against them before they realize the money from their crops, bankruptcy and ruin will be the fate of hundreds."

Eben Davis had kept afloat in 1866. By the summer of 1867, how-ever, when it became apparent (because of excessive rain and worms) that the year's crop would again be a disaster, his creditors could wait no longer. In August, he was forced to declare bankruptcy in the Dis-trict Court of the Northern District of Mississippi. Among his thirty-seven creditors were kin, neighbors, the Citizens Bank of Louisiana, attorneys, physicians, druggists, and merchants in Holly Springs, Memphis, and New Orleans. The largest sum owed was $9450 still due the estate of Roger Barton on Davis's 1859 note for purchase of the Barton plantation running north of Strawberry Plains to the Coldwater River. Next came $7769 owed the estate of Capt. E. P. Kilpatrick, a nearby planter. Almost $6000 had been borrowed from Davis's sister-in-law, Mary Jane Greenlee Finley. That was followed closely by the amount owned the Louisiana bank, and the list con-tinued down a long column. The Barton heirs found the most imme-diate redress; they regained title to their father's land. Other creditors would either never be paid, or they would wait for years as various Davis properties came on the auction block. On February 17, 1868, at a forced sale of the Strawberry Plains plantation on the courthouse steps, George J. Finley stepped forward and purchased the place for $2800. The ties of blood held strong, and the careful Finleys had come forward to save their Davis kin. After the Finleys took title, they allowed the Davises to continue to farm the original 640 acres purchased in 1837, but from this point onward the Finleys farmed the 320 acres adjoining the McKissack place that had been added to Strawberry Plains in 1845. This was the first step in a long chain of mortgages and sales through which the Finley family eventually came to own and control the entire Audubon Center tract.[11]

The disastrous cotton crop had ruined many. The letters of the Scales family at nearby Oakland plantation reflect the general situation at the end of 1867. "You never saw such a *blue* set as the farmers in this region in your life. Everybody is *broken*, we among the rest," wrote one member. "Indeed I have heard the cry of 'Hard Times' so much that the words actually form themselves into a 'Misere' as the wind moans so dismally (yet not unmusically) around the old house at night." Only the Finleys stood now between the Davises and destitution. In his mid-teens, Johnny Davis was taken out of school to help his father in farming. He would eventually become the primary support of his extended family. The well-educated Finley women, however, saw to it that the three Davis daughters went to Franklin Female Academy, the sole girls school in Holly Springs to survive the war. They would not allow their cousins to miss the educational advantages for women to which the town had been committed since its founding.[12]

Fortunately the cotton crops of 1868 and 1869 signaled a turn for the better. Still the 1870 agricultural census reveals that Eben Davis had produced in the preceding year only nineteen bales of cotton, in comparison with the four hundred bales harvested in 1860. The glory days of King Cotton were not to return to Strawberry Plains. In contrast, George J. Finley and his mother together had a yield of fifty-six bales.[13]

The cautious Finleys, constitutionally indisposed to indebtedness, had come out of the war solvent and had begun to add to their capital. The affairs of the family were very complicated because the majority of their assets were held in common. As eldest son, George functioned as head of the family finances for forty years. Of the daughters, the two eldest, Virginia and Emma, were spinsters living at Woodland with their mother in 1870. The youngest, Augusta, had married a Holly Springs merchant and former Confederate, Maj. Lewis Scruggs, shortly after the war. In the late 1860s both sons also married.[14]

They took different paths both in marriage and in matters of business. In 1868 George Finley married his country neighbor and childhood sweetheart, Nannie Dunlap, daughter of Dr. Thomas Dunlap, a rock-ribbed Scots Presbyterian even more conservative than the Finleys. Leaving the home plantation to his mother and sisters, at his marriage George built a comfortable brick cottage on some family land on Salem Road to the east and north of Holly Springs and only three or four miles southeast of Strawberry Plains. From that seat, he established himself as one of the county's most capable farmers. In 1869 his brother John Finley married Betsy Hull, quite a different kind of young lady, who added color and sometimes drama to the Finley skein. She was the daughter of John Hull and Anne Crump, representatives of intertwined Virginia families from Fredericksburg, proud, aristocratic, and sometimes controversial Episcopalians. Betsy's uncle William Crump had remained pro-Union while all his sons were serving in the Confederate Army. His sister, Betsy's widowed mother, a loyal Confederate, was a spirited woman. Writing in the middle of the war to her sister back in Virginia, Mrs. Hull reported the loss of most of her property, told about her experiences in running the blockade to Memphis, and expressed her sense of the future: "I feel sorry for the young people, deprived of every privilege, even without education which might enable them to make a living. My children had a bright prospect, but poverty awaits them now. I think when the war is over, I shall keep a big hotel somewhere." Later in the letter she explained that she had already been keeping a sort of family hotel for the large connection during the war and might as well get paid for it. Even after the war, however, she continued to indulge her children. In 1866 a contemporary reported of her daughters Susan and Betsy: "They don't think of anything but dress, fashion, & beaux, & dress *finer now* than they ever did. They have a good many parties & seem to enjoy themselves a *great deal*." Three years later when she married John Finley, Betsy was still the belle, longing for the life of fashion. She would prove a colorful figure later in the increasingly convoluted history of the Audubon Center lands. Upon his marriage, John moved into the Hull home in Holly Springs. John was generous of spirit and one of most popular young men of the town, but he did not have the Finley business acumen of his older brother, George. In 1869 he purchased from George the half section of Eben Davis's land adjoining the McKissack place, but he was forced to mortgage it more than once in the ensuing years. In the 1870s, he went into the dry goods business for a time in partnership with his brothers-in-law Lewis Scruggs and Brodie Hull and his wife's cousin James M. Crump. Afterward he was involved in other ventures, the final one calamitous.[15]

In 1875, seven years after the Finleys had purchased Strawberry Plains to save it for the Davis family, the Davises were able to buy back the original 640 acres. Using the fees from his levee work, Eben Davis Jr. paid sixteen hundred dollars for the north 243 acres. The remaining 397 acres on which the house stood George Finley sold to Martha Greenlee Davis and her younger son, John Presley Davis, in exchange for Martha's one-seventh interest in the Greenlee's Ferry tract in Rockbridge County, Virginia. The Davises once again owned their homestead. They had regained a measure of stability.[16]

10

THE FREEDMEN AND STRAWBERRY PLAINS BAPTIST CHURCH

THE TEN YEARS following the Civil War were a time of political and social struggle, as well as economic uncertainty. The state constitutional convention, which assembled in the summer of 1865, nullified the ordinance of secession, declared that "the institution of slavery having been destroyed in the State of Mississippi, neither slavery nor involuntary servitude . . . shall hereafter exist in this State," and set for the fall the election of a provisional government. The subsequently elected legislature, however, surprisingly enacted the controversial Black Code, severely limiting the rights of the freedmen. Many leaders, such as former Confederate Senator J. W. C. Watson of Holly Springs, felt that the body had "gone much too far." They were correct. An outcry arose in the north that Mississippi was attempting to reinstitute slavery, and the Republican majority in the U.S. Congress passed the Reconstruction Act of 1867, which placed Mississippi under the rule of U.S. military forces and granted freedmen the right to vote. The first biracial election, held in the fall of 1867, swept into power a newly constructed Republican Party run by an amalgam of carpetbaggers, lately come down from the North; scalawags, as white political converts were called; and local African American leaders, many of them ministers. This Republican organization was kept in power by appealing to a bloc of freedmen voters until 1875, when the Democratic Party regained control of the state.[1]

Two organizations greatly intensified the level of anxiety between the races. The first was the Loyal League. Begun in 1867 by northern whites and blacks as a means to insure the freedmen's loyalty to the Republican Party, the clubs held barbeques and dances and sponsored solidarity-celebrating parades that were particularly threatening to the white population, who were in great fear of armed insurrection. The processions in Holly Springs, which seemed to some observers a mile long, were led by freedmen wearing red oilcloth caps with red feathers, red sashes, and enormous red and blue badges and carrying flaming torches. But the most unsettling feature to the whites was the companies of drummers. A hundred years later, a Davis granddaughter recalled being told of the "night marches organized by the 'carpetbaggers'" in the years following the war: "Every night at sundown drums were beaten, and the marchers gathered together to light torches and roam through the countryside in a show of force." The children who grew up at Strawberry Plains in these postwar years would long remember sleepless nights punctuated by the terrifying sounds.[2]

In 1868 came the organization of dens of the Ku Klux Klan in the state and in the county. In the minds of many former slaves, the Klan seemed a postwar incarnation of the hated slave patrollers. According to the early historian of Marshall reconstruction, a major objective of the dens was the disarming of all freedman. Such raids are well described by a former slave in neighboring Lafayette County: "Atter de war cum de Ku Klux; dey didn't cum to my house 'cause dey wuz lookin fur niggers wid guns; all de niggers had bot guns wid de money dey wuz paid fur workin'; dey jus' wanted dem to hunt rabbits an' sich but de Ku Klux didn't want dem to hav' guns; dey wud hide out in de swamp, but sumhow de Ku Klux knew ever' thing dey did or said; dey mus' had a pilot; dey wud take deir guns away frum dem an' run dem out ov de swamp. De Ku Klux rid on horses an' de men's an' de hosses had on uniforms . . . an' dey sed dey wux de speerits ov de soldiers dat were killed at Shiloh." In addition, under cover of darkness the Klan made visits to intimidate freedmen they considered troublemakers. It has been maintained that the local cells did not resort to burning property or "deeds of extreme violence." According to testimony before the congressional Boutwell Committee, which investigated the Klan in the 1870s, Marshall County "whites and blacks alike were quiet and orderly in comparison with other counties." One whipping of a black man, however, was noted in the report, and there must have been others.[3]

Beneath the dramatic and disruptive political and social machinations of the period lay the desperate plight of the freed slaves. Largely illiterate and unskilled, they had gained their freedom but found themselves in an immediate economic limbo. Through the late months of 1865, masses waited for the U.S. government to provide them with a new start by the gift of forty acres and a mule. Though the origin of that legend is unclear today, the distribution was widely expected for months following Appomattox. "Lots of the colored folks had false ideas concerning freedom," former slave and Baptist preacher Edward Jones commented. "They thought they were going to be on top and govern the country, and the Yankees would confirm that idea. It was natural for them to say that 'cause they were fighting against the South. It was many a long day before they got it all straightened out." He added, "It didn't bother me none. I just went on farming." Such was the case with freedmen in the Strawberry Plains neighborhood. Their most pressing concern was making a living.[4]

Many freedmen were in dire need. Planter Robert B. Alexander records in his June 1865 diary finding a black woman with five children at the Holly Springs depot begging to "work for milk and bread." Several days later he reported that a neighbor had hired three "contrabands" (the term given slaves runaway to the Union Army) at forty cents per day for the men and twenty-five cents for the woman. By fall the Freedmen's Bureau had been established in Holly Springs and was overseeing contracts. The standard form issued for the bureau in 1865, headed "Agreement with Freedmen," specifies that the landowner "agrees to furnish to the said laborers and those rightfully dependent upon them free of charge, clothing and food of good quality and sufficient quantity; good and sufficient quarters, medical attendance when necessary and kind and humane treatment; to exempt from the lands of the said plantation, for garden purposes, one acre to each family; such allotment to include a reasonable uses of tools and animals for the cultivation of the same, to exact only one half a day labor on Saturdays, and none whatever on Sundays." Space was provided immediately following for recording specific terms of payment. On one such a contract, dated October 7, 1865, was added in script that the landowner "further agrees to give him fifty dollars for cultivating sayd lands & he further agrees to give him one suit of cloths." A printed clause toward the end of the document states that if the landowner shall fail to meet the agreed terms "or be guilty of cruelty, he shall, besides the legal recourse left to the party or parties aggrieved, render this contract liable to annulment by the Provost Marshal of Freedman." The workers were not to be required to work more than ten hours a day in summer and nine in winter. If the worker "shall neglect or refuse to perform the labor herein promised," he is to be subject to punishment by the Provost Marshall of Freedman. The document concludes, "It is further agreed that any wages or share of profit due the said laborer under this agreement, shall constitute a first lien upon all crops or parts of crops produced on said plantation or tract of land by their labor. And no shipments of products shall be made until the Provost Marshal of Freedman shall certify that all dues to said laborers are paid or satisfactorily arranged." At the close of 1865 the Freedmen's Bureau ceased to exercise authority over the labor contracts, but continued to see that the rights of freedman were protected and to aid them in prosecuting their grievances in court. The bureau also served as a clearinghouse for labor disputes. On October 31, 1868, E. N. Davis filed a grievance against two of his workers, Landon Davis and Charley Burnett. The bureau proceedings read: "Davis made complaint that Landon and Charley will not work and are neglecting their crop. Reprimanded Landon and gave authority to Davis to discharge Burnett and to allow him proceeds of his portion of crop up to date."[5]

By this time, the Freedmen's Bureau for the Holly Springs district was reporting that most county freedmen were entering into one of three kinds of work agreement: wage labor at fifteen dollars a month, labor for one-third of the crop and their subsistence, and labor for one-half the crop "and subsist themselves." In time, wage labor came to represent an increasingly small percentage of the agreements, and ten years after the war, farming on shares or sharecropping had emerged as the primary form of tenancy.[6]

Sharecropping marked the end of the plantation system. Resisting a return to any vestige of slavery, the freedmen wanted their own dwellings, not communal quarters; they objected to the plantation's gang labor even for wages; and they sought to be free from constant supervision. The rise of the sharecropping system resulted in the division of plantations into farming units of between thirty and fifty acres operated by individual black families. Sharecropping, although far from a perfect solution to the South's underlying economic problems, represented at the time the best alternative for both the freedman and the landowner, in the words of historian James L. Roark, "the primary means of bringing together landowners without capital and laborers without land." The system became so much a part of the culture that when freedmen began buying land in the neighborhood in the late 1870s, the more prosperous of them had sharecroppers.[7]

Marshall County sharecroppers in a cotton field. Courtesy of the Dean Collection, University of Mississippi

While landowners and freedmen were working out mutually acceptable financial arrangements, the Freedmen's Bureau was also encouraging efforts to educate African Americans. Typically these initiatives, often supported by northern religious groups, were centered in the towns, and more than one school was begun in Holly Springs. But these early efforts had no immediate or far-reaching effects on country neighborhoods. Instead, the organization that immediately became the center of neighborhood life and remains a powerful force to this day issued from the neighboring freedmen themselves. In 1867, while they were still struggling to gain some sort of economic stability, a small group of the vicinity's freed slaves founded a church.[8]

Of the history of religious effort among the area's slaves, we have some outlines. An earlier chapter dealt with the establishment in 1845 by whites of Wesley Chapel a couple of miles northwest of Strawberry Plains and presented documentary evidence that slaves attended both the Sunday services and camp meetings with their masters. The Davises were among the early members. Another church, Fairview Cumberland Presbyterian, was built in 1850 on the Seal plantation immediately south of Strawberry Plains. The small congregation, which included the Seal, Stephenson, McWilliams, and Cochran families, probably met only monthly. Slaves may well have gone to services there also. The Wesley Chapter Register, however, contains no slave members, and the Fairview roll is not extant. The one church in the far reaches of the neighborhood that did have slave members was Pleasant Grove Baptist Church, five miles to the west on the William Clayton plantation. Among the charter members in 1848 was Harriet, "a colored sister." In 1866, when the church sponsored the organization of separate congregation for African Americans, it had a membership of 108, of whom 66 were freedmen. Several of them had been slaves on what had become known as the Dawson plantation in 1854, when Mrs. Eliza Perkins Williams married her third husband, Senator William C. Dawson of Georgia.[9]

Col. Eben Davis's granddaughter spoke once to me of a church for the Davis slaves on Strawberry Plains, but the organization was probably not a formal one. Likely the slaves merely gathered periodically under a brush arbor or in some farm building to hear a preacher, whose denominational affiliation and race are not now known. Despite efforts of white ministers (and often because these ministers so often emphasized obedience to white masters), slaves evolved their own form of Christianity. At the camp meetings, they "outshouted" the whites and stayed up far into night praying and singing hymns to which they brought their own cadence and rhythm, drawing upon the African call-and-response pattern. Many of the churches that the freedmen founded immediately after the war were Baptist. But it has been said that the slaves were only superficially fundamentalist, whereas "the whites were fiery mad," the "blacks were fiery glad." Historian Eugene Genovese has maintained, "African tradition imparted to the religion of the slaves an irrepressible affirmation of life." They could at the same time both see "the world as a 'vale of tears' and yet experience a joy in life that has sometimes evoked admiration from whites, sometimes contempt, but almost always astonishment."[10]

It is puzzling why when the neighborhood church was organized in 1867 on Mt. Pleasant Road, it was named Strawberry Plains Baptist Church, since it met on land owned by Mrs. Dawson adjoining the Davis holding. Perhaps the fact that the Davis family did not actually own Strawberry Plains at the time (the Finleys did) explains why the freedmen had to rely on Mrs. Dawson to provide them a site. Or perhaps the explanation is simpler. The Davis plantation did not have frontage on Mt. Pleasant Road, and access would have been through the Dawson land anyway. So Mrs. Dawson simply allowed the church to use the sliver of her land that lay east of the road adjoining Strawberry Plains. The naming, however, suggests that the members saw their church as a continuation of the pre–Civil War religious organization on the Davis plantation.

Though no roster of the original members survives, we do know the founding church officials, the deacons, and church mothers: Frank Lee, Matt Finley, Allen Perkins, Joe Oliver, Tom Williams, Martha Jane Perkins, Sally Stephenson, and Fannie Wall Lawrence. All were young, in their twenties and thirties, and all were connected with the three antebellum plantations converging near the church site—Strawberry Plains, the Williams-Dawson plantation, and the Stephenson place.[11]

Most were well-known figures in the neighborhood. Frank Lee spent most of his life on Strawberry Plains. He and his wife, Margaret, were the stalwart support of Martha Greenlee Davis during the war and after, and they were spoken of with the greatest respect and affection even a hundred years later. Matt Finley must have been a former Finley slave sent up to look after Finley interests after the Davis bankruptcy. The other three founding deacons—Tom Williams, Allen Perkins, and Joe Oliver—had 'all grown up on the Williams-Dawson plantation, and Tom is perhaps the Dawson slave listed only by his given name on the roll of Pleasant Grove Baptist Church. Allen Perkins and his wife, Martha Jane, are both designated mulatto in the 1880 census, and Allen was one of the first African Americans to own land in the immediate area. Joe Oliver would also become a landowner. In 1871 he married Leatha Stephenson, by whom he had nine children—Moses Flavus, Felix Stedon, Milton Henry, Wright, the twins Willie and Lillie, Fred Person, Savannah, and Allen. Probably no African American family was held in higher esteem by all members of this community, black and white.[12]

The remaining two founding church mothers were also long important presences. Fannie Wall Lawrence was a large, imposing, very dark woman who lived into her nineties—a formidable person until the end. She was likely born on one of the Wall plantations located several miles to the east—Sunnyside or Cloverlands. Her husband, Henry Lawrence, was apparently born on Maj. Stephenson's plantation, where he was living in 1880, though Fannie and her children were then living on Strawberry Plains. Sally Stephenson was born April 10, 1845, on the Stephenson plantation and died there in 1902. She was a house servant during the Civil War and remained as cook for four generations of the Stephenson family. According to census records she never married, but she reared a number of children, including her mulatto nephew Zeek Stephenson.[13]

These founding leaders of Strawberry Plains Baptist Church were established, productive citizens who had the respect of the white landowners. That is made apparent by the way in which the trustees first gained title to the church land. Because the trustees were illiterate and without credit, a white middleman of the neighborhood bought the tract for them to secure a clear title. Mrs. Eliza Perkins Williams Dawson had died in 1874 without making a will, and her large estate was divided among her siblings and their heirs. The portion adjoining Strawberry Plains fell to her nephew Newton Cannon and his brother and sister. On December 22, 1879, in Williamson County, Tennessee, the Cannons sold to William R. Cox, the former overseer who had married Maj. Stephenson's widow, for the sum of ninety dollars, four acres east of Mt. Pleasant Road in the northeast corner of Section 14. A month later, Cox conveyed the tract to the church for the same sum. The congregation now owned land and could build a church, called affectionately simply "Strawberry," that would be a spiritual and cultural force for scores of years.[14]

11

THE NEXT GENERATION

O N JANUARY 15, 1881, a black-bordered funeral notice was distributed around the Holly Springs square and within the immediate country neighborhoods, inviting "The friends and acquaintances of the late E. N. Davis" to attend his funeral "from the residence 5 miles North of Holly Springs at 2 o'clock tomorrow." Four years later, in February, another black-bordered notice announced the funeral of Mary Jane Finley at the Holly Springs Presbyterian Church, where the clerk noted in the register that she was the oldest member of the congregation. The pioneer generation was passing, and the next generation had already taken the reigns of family affairs. George Finley had assumed management for his family before the war, and Johnny Davis had shouldered his family's burden since the Davises bought most of Strawberry Plains back from the Finleys in 1875.[1]

For many decades, John Presley Davis provided the main support for an extended family, which included at various times his mother, brother, two sisters, and their husbands and children. Although he did it without complaint and was much beloved for his generous spirit and sweet nature, his brave efforts were plagued by forces outside his control. As his niece later said of him, "Every time Uncle Johnny got on his feet, something would come along to knock him off of them again."[2]

Things started off well enough for the Davises in 1875. The second daughter, Ann Winifred (called Nannie), had just married, much to the family's joy, her cousin Presley Stanback. He had moved from North Carolina to farm family land south of Byhalia in Marshall County, so Nannie was well settled not too far away. Eben Jr. was making enough from his levee work to treat his younger brother to

George James Finley (1834–1910) as a young man. Courtesy of the Audubon Mississippi/Strawberry Plains Finley Collection, University of Mississippi

John Presley Davis (1851–1927) as a young man. Courtesy of the Audubon Mississippi/Strawberry Plains Finley Collection, University of Mississippi

a trip to the Centennial Fair in Philadelphia in 1876 and to buy 160 acres of the Barton plantation in 1877. But the marriage the next year of the youngest daughter, Augusta (Gussie), was another matter. Long remembered as a great beauty, she was the petted darling of the family. Gussie had fallen in love with the handsome, dark-eyed Dempsey Brittenum, son of an established landed family of Mt. Pleasant, a few miles north. The year before the marriage, he had inherited the large, productive Gibbons plantation—the eastern-most tract of what is now the Audubon Center and the site during the Civil War of the Coldwater camp. But Demps was cavalier with money and restless. "Gussie married last spring much against my wishes and her father sided with me, but her mother & sisters either favored the match or did not make any opposition," George Finley wrote his uncle in Virginia. By the summer of 1879, Gussie and her infant son had moved back to Strawberry Plains while Demps continued to indulge his wanderlust. "She is much dispirited and has grieved much," George reported, "but [is] too proud to complain as she told her father at the time of her marriage that she would marry Brittenum in spite of him and the world." Gussie would continue to live at the family homestead supported by her brother for the next twenty years.[3]

Demps Brittenum was born a generation too late, for he would probably have made a dashing and gallant soldier in the Civil War. His finest hour, in fact, came during another of the great testing times in Marshall County history—the yellow fever epidemic of 1878. At the end of a particularly wet summer, when residents were noting an abundance of mosquitoes, yellow fever broke out in New Orleans and was carried up the railroad as far as Grenada, Mississippi, just eighty miles south of Holly Springs. "Yellow Jack" had never touched the town, which the citizenry had long considered so high and "salubrious" as to be safe from danger. In a chivalric, ill-fated gesture, leading citizens persuaded the town fathers to open the village to refugees from the south. Within a few days, fever was declared epidemic in "the city of flowers." Of the 1440 people stricken, 304 died before the first frost came. Among the selfless and noble heroes of the plague were members of the Howard Association, an organization formed of doctors and laymen who ministered to the stricken during yellow fever epidemics. Active in the Holly Springs association

Ginning season at the Strawberry Plains gin. Courtesy of the Audubon Mississippi/Strawberry Plains Finley Collection, University of Mississippi

was Demps Brittenum, who would be remembered best by some for his courage and sacrifices during the fever.[4]

Unlike the war, this scourge was contained in the town, where virtually every merchant on the square was left bankrupt. This time, however, the farmers of the surrounding countryside did not suffer the same economic ruin. At Strawberry Plains, Johnny Davis continued slowly expanding his farming operation, adding a cotton gin again to the plantation grouping. The late 1880s, however, dealt the Davises many blows. In the spring of 1885, Eben Jr. was seriously injured in the collision of two passenger trains in the central part of the state, one leg crushed and the other severely bruised. He was brought up the railroad to John and Betsy Finley's home in Holly Springs. Though the doctors advised amputation, Martha Greenlee Davis refused to allow it and devoted herself to nursing him. Over time he was able to walk with only a slight limp, but his days of working were over. "I am sorry to hear of Martha's afflictions," her brother John F. Greenlee had written his niece Virginia Finley. "Some people have all the ease & comfort in life that the world can give, while others have the sorrows and afflictions."[5]

Hauling cotton bales from the Strawberry Plains gin. Courtesy of the Audubon Mississippi/Strawberry Plains Finley Collection, University of Mississippi

Eben's accident had economic repercussions, for he was now forced to sell his land and settle his affairs, and Johnny Davis had to raise the money to buy it. But the greatest financial blow came from another source. Dempsey Brittenum died in 1885, and a year and a half later, Gussie married Robert Johnson, another charmer, who convinced Johnny to go into partnership with him and invest in land and a gin in Arkansas. To everyone's distress, Johnson turned out to be a compulsive gambler who embezzled funds from the partnership. Everything came to a head for John Davis at the beginning of 1890. It is dispiriting to read through the poor young man's financial records. First, he bought and immediately mortgaged to George Finley the 243 acres Eben Jr. owned of Strawberry Plains. The next day, John and his mother mortgaged everything—the 397 acres of Strawberry Plains on which the house stood, their stock, a house and gin in Forest City, Arkansas, and land in Poinsett County, Arkansas. The decade was just beginning of what a local historian characterized as "the lean years of the nineties" and "the hard times of five cent cotton." At the time, a nearby planter spoke of the period as "the hardest times in this county [I] ever saw" and noted that, because of economic distress, numbers of people were leaving the county and moving to Texas. During the lean nineties, the Davises lost all of the mortgaged Arkansas property.[6]

Meanwhile Johnny Davis struggled to hold on to Strawberry Plains and support his family. The decade did finally see Gussie rewarded with a happy marriage. Robert Johnson died in 1895, and two years later Gussie, now three years short of forty, married her third husband, her first cousin Judge Clarence Greenlee of Brinkley, Arkansas, a distinguished attorney and one of the largest landowners in that state. Though Gussie, now wealthy and secure, left Strawberry Plains, her son by Demps Brittenum remained. Coming also to live there were another sister and her family, so Johnny Davis actually became responsible for even more kin. The 1900 census shows him as head of a household consisting of his mother; his brother Eben; his oldest, sweetest, plainest sister, Mary (who had married at almost forty a man seven years her junior and not a success); Mary's husband, Charles Moseley; his five-year-old niece, Martha Moseley; his twenty-one-year-old nephew, Roger Brittenum; and two servants.[7]

George Finley, like his cousin, also had problems with his own family. Two of his sisters, Emma Finley and Augusta Finley Scruggs, died in 1877. In addition to managing the settlement of their estates (the second of which was encumbered by the debts of his brother-in-law, Lewis Scruggs) and the estate of his wife's father, Dr. Thomas Dunlap, George became guardian of his nephew Finley Scruggs. The nephew proved a handful, and the family tried various solutions to settle him down. In 1881 George's younger brother John commented wryly from southern Mississippi, "If Finley had been sent down here, he would have had no Saloons or Billiard Halls to hang around." But Finley had not been subdued when Mary Jane Greenlee Finley died at Woodland in 1885, or when John Finley died in Holly Springs unexpectedly in 1889.[8]

"Great hearted, generous, and true, firm in his friendships and faithful to all," the Holly Springs *Reporter* characterized John Finley in its eulogy. "All business houses were closed and schools suspended to attend the funeral, which was the largest that has ever taken place in our town." John had died at the age of thirty-five. Though the most widely mourned of his family, John lacked the Finley caution and judgment. He had tried a number of endeavors. At his marriage, he had become a merchant on the southern side of the square on the site of his father's Union House, which had been destroyed in Van Dorn's raid. Ten years later he was working for the Mississippi Valley Company in southern Mississippi as a dealer in longleaf pine lumber, and in 1885 family and friends secured him the position of Holly Springs postmaster. Unfortunately, just the year before his death he went deeply into debt in founding the Alabama and Pennsylvania Improvement Company to purchase and develop four thousand acres on the Tennessee River in Decatur County, Tennessee. On the day of his death, John dictated a brief will leaving everything to his wife, Betsy, but the responsibility for managing his estate and dealing with the indebtedness incurred in the Tennessee venture fell to his brother, George.[9]

To help support John's family, George Finley, Johnny Davis, and several prominent townsmen successfully petitioned to have Betsy fill her husband's position as postmaster for the remaining year of the term. George was doing his best for his brother's widow, but Betsy Hull Finley, the Civil War era belle, was strong willed and assertive. So colorful a Holly Springs personage did she become that she would be the subject of a sketch by a local writer published in the *Atlantic Monthly*:

> This vivacious lady, forty years old, the mother of [six] children, has the brightest eyes, the gayest laugh, and the longest widow's veil in [town]. Since her husband's death . . . she has always worn the deepest mourning, but a life of seclusion seems undesirable and inexpedient for more than a short twelve-month. She goes everywhere—to all the entertainments, dances, baseball games, Woman's Auxiliary meetings; to church every time the bell rings; even to the Philharmonic Society, though she is careful to explain that she's not a bit literary. Irreverent boys . . . say that a dog-fight can't begin until [she] gets there. She makes all the clothes worn by herself and her . . . children, except the boys' suits after the boys are ten years old; she raises flowers and vegetables that would make a country fair blush for shame; she is an incessant talker, and a notable cook. When called

upon to contribute a cake, a salad, or a bucket of lye-hominy for a
church supper, she never makes an excuse; she always has time for
everything.

After visiting Holly Springs during this period, the Georgia humor-
ist Bill Arp described it as "an old fashioned town" where before the
war much "wealth and refinement had its abode." But now he commented, "the wealth is largely diminished, and without it even refinement has to struggle to retain its prestige." Betsy was still an aristo-
crat (make no mistake about that!), and she could energetically adjust
to hard times while maintaining her relish and gaiety. But she also felt
that the Finley family had a continuing obligation to her. After carrying the debts of John Finley's estate for a number of years, George
Finley finally asked that Betsy settle with him. He offered to take as
payment title to that part of Strawberry Plains north of the McKissack plantation (which her husband had bought in 1868). Her re-
sponse was spirited and definite: "I have often heard [my husband]
say all of his sister Emma's estate went to pay Mr. Scruggs' debt &
that he [Mr. Scruggs] owed you. I also heard you say that Mr. Dunlap owed you & still his family got their portion when the Dunlap
estate was sold. It seems right hard that I am the only one held responsible for old debts." She further insisted, "after the first few
years of my inexperience when I was first married," her husband's
debts "were not of my making but of unfortunate business ventures
of which I did not approve." That settled the matter, and Betsy still
held the land at her death.[10]

George Finley had better luck with investments he made on his
own than he did with these family affairs. With the care and planning that many associated with the Finley name, he steadily made
his way in the world and added to his own estate. He was a progressive farmer. In his extensive financial records, subscriptions to *Prac-
tical Farmer* and *Southern Cultivator* take their place amid bills for
clothes for his wife and children and receipts from the George Dickel
distillery. In the 1890s, he became closely involved with the Mississippi Agricultural Experiment Station at Starkville and volunteered
some of his farmland for their test studies of fertilizers. He regularly
attended meetings of the Mississippi Farmers Institute, and in 1893

he was appointed by Gov. John Marshall Stone as delegate to the National Farmers Congress. That year he paid taxes on six sections of land, which included the Finley estate, his wife's share of the Dunlap holdings, and land he had purchased in his own name. He had also gone into a farming partnership with H. O. Rand, a Holly Springs cotton buyer. The partnership had purchased the old Gibbons plantation (which the Gibbons heirs had sold to the Puryear family and that had, in turn, been inherited and then lost by Mrs. Puryear's brother, Demps Brittenum). At the end of 1899, George bought out the undivided half interest of Rand's heirs in the thousand-acre plantation. The easternmost tract of the present Audubon Center was now in Finley hands.[11]

It was also at this time that the McKissack plantation, lying between the Gibbons place and Strawberry Plains, first came under Finley management. Like those of all Marshall planters, Capt. Alexander McKissack's farming operations were greatly reduced after the war. On the 1860 agricultural census schedules, he is credited with producing eighty-six bales of cotton. That figure had fallen to twelve bales by 1870. He and his wife, who were childless, lived a quiet existence on their secluded plantation. In noting a visit to his family back in Spring Hill, Tennessee, the Columbia *Herald and Mail* described Capt. McKissack as "a gentleman of fine intellect and the ripest scholarship." Making allowance for Southern Victorian grandiloquence, still he was a graduate of Yale, and in Marshall County he was judged "a refined, highly educated, polished gentleman." In 1898 this "unobtrusive citizen" died in Memphis from a heart condition while visiting his sister, Mrs. Jessie Helen McKissack Peters, who held a mortgage on her brother's Coldwater plantation.[12]

And so the passionate Jessie reenters our history, again leaving tragedy and scandal in her wake. The events leading up to the murder of Van Dorn by her husband, Dr. George Boddie Peters, are matched in drama by the subsequent McKissack-Peters history. After killing Van Dorn on May 7, 1863, in Spring Hill, Tennessee, Dr. Peters was a fugitive until that fall, when he was arrested by a Confederate force in the Mississippi Delta, where he was hiding at the home of his niece Mrs. Thomas McNeill (the former "Pidge" Arthur of Holly Springs). Tried and acquitted (probably because the military court considered his motivation a matter of personal honor), Peters then crossed the river and exiled himself in Arkansas. Back at Spring Hill, on January 26, 1864, eight and a half months after the murder, his estranged wife Jessie gave birth to a daughter, whom she named Medora. The year after the war, Dr. Peters brought suit for divorce in Arkansas, claiming that he had been "deserted by his wife on May 7, 1863." Within a year, his son Thomas Peters, in despair over the Van Dorn murder, took his own life in Memphis, and subsequently Thomas's sister Clara fled to St. Louis and entered a convent.[13]

In the name of all decency, the story should then have come to an end. But it did not. Dr. Peters made the newspapers again when a man in Arkansas attempted to kill him by firing a derringer, and the doctor cut the man's throat with a penknife. Gruesome as that was, it scarcely attracted the attention that did this notice in the July 9, 1868, issue of the Nashville *Republican Banner*: "Dr. Peters, widely known as the man who shot and killed General Van Dorn of the Confederate Army, during the war, for alleged intimacy with Mrs. Peters, was in this city one day this week in company with the quondam Mrs. P. The long estranged couple are now said to be on the best of terms, and it is reported that the broken marriage vows are soon to be renewed." The report was correct. Dr. Peters and Jessie were remarried, had three more children, and settled in Memphis. Dr. Peters died at age seventy-four in 1889 and was interred in Elmwood Cemetery. Nine years later Jessie's brother Capt. Alexander McKissack was buried in the same plot.[14]

A brief coda still remains to the story. In the early 1960s, a woman attending a meeting of the Civil War Roundtable in Jackson, Mississippi, revealed to military historian Edwin Bearss that she was the granddaughter of Medora Peters. She told him that, within the family, it was acknowledged that Medora was the daughter of Gen. Van Dorn.[15]

Jessie McKissack's name was first associated with the McKissack plantation on the Coldwater River when she was a girl of seventeen and one of the co-heirs to the property. It was last linked when she was a woman of nearly seventy, who held a mortgage on the plantation. In the interval what a mark she had made! By the time she gave up all claim to the property, it was under the control of George Finley. Upon Capt. McKissack's death in 1898, his widow appointed Finley executor of the estate and turned over to him management of the McKissack land. By the end of the century, George Finley was farming both plantations to the east of Strawberry Plains.[16]

12

A NEW CENTURY

THE TWENTIETH CENTURY opened on a changing economic and cultural landscape in the region south of the Coldwater River. Postal service and the telephone had now come to the neighborhood. In 1894 Maj. Stephenson's grandson Edward L. McAlexander secured a post office for a general store he had opened in the major's plantation office, and residents of the area, including the Davises at Strawberry Plains, had their mail sent to Mack, Mississippi. In the summer of 1898, McAlexander added to the old office a long room fronting Mt. Pleasant Road. A telephone was installed soon afterward, the only one for miles. The store and post office at Mack provided a hub and gave a name to the community.[1]

During the same period Mack School was built for the white children of Coldwater. E. L. McAlexander was trustee, and the teacher boarded at the Stephenson-McAlexander house. It was always a small school, with never more than twenty students enrolled. Among the students in 1900 were the five oldest McAlexander children and Johnny Davis's niece, six-year-old Martha Moseley.[2]

Mack School, however, was the second school in the neighborhood. In 1892 under a separate-but-equal incentive, a building where African Americans could be educated was erected half a mile to the south, close by Strawberry Plains Baptist Church on Mt. Pleasant Road. Strawberry School was a two-story, tin-roofed, rough-framed structure resting upon huge logs set on sandstone boulders. The first year, 489 students enrolled, among them Hunts, Howells, Harrises, Lees, Davises, Perkinses, Olivers, Stephensons, and Bagleys. All students were in the first grade. This was the first opportunity given them for an education, and boys and girls of nineteen and twenty came with their much younger brothers and sisters to learn to read and write. By 1900, the enrollment had grown to 546 children.[3]

In 1905 the structure housing Strawberry Church was destroyed by fire, and two years later the congregation, which had now grown to more than two hundred members, built a new church. The frame building was entered by two doors, the one on the right for men and that on the left for women and children. The church bell, hung in a low tower above the front vestibule, was used as a means of communication for African Americans in the neighborhood. One member especially chosen (for a long time Zeek Stephenson) was allowed to ring the bell, which pealed loudly and mournfully through the countryside to announced a death. The tolling continued until the churchyard was filled with folk from the surrounding fields come to learn of the arrangements for the burial in one of the three cemeteries for blacks dating from the days of slavery—one on the Dawson place, one on the Stephenson place at Mack, and one on Strawberry Plains. For decades people in the community were summoned by the bell, and for seventy years the church structure stood as a important landmark along Mt. Pleasant Road.[4]

The establishment of Strawberry Church in 1867 had been just one step in the progress of the African American community. In December 1880, Allen Perkins, a founding deacon of the church, became the first freedman to buy land in the neighborhood, purchasing acreage south of the church from the Dawson estate. Gradually a few others were able to buy small farms. But a few miles to the north, an African American success story was developing so dramatically that it entered local folklore. In 1893 an enterprising young mulatto named James Holmes Teer purchased, "for cash in hand," a tract of 250 acres on the northern bank of the Coldwater. Legend would have it that he bought the land with a pot of gold he had discovered while putting in fence posts. Whatever the source of the money, Teer proved a remarkably able farmer, who rapidly amassed a large landholding. By 1900 he had bought all of Section 26 along the Coldwater, 640 acres, and he was leasing it to sharecroppers. Eventually he would own a tract of 2305 acres, a gin and a grist mill on Coldwater, and a store building in Holly Springs. Wearing a white hat and dressed in a tie, he rode over his acres daily supervising the workers, it is said on white horses, one during the morning and another in the afternoon. In 1905 Teer was instrumental in helping another local man born in slavery, the Rev. Elias Cottrell, now a bishop of the Colored Methodist Church, to realize his dream of establishing a college for his race in Holly Springs. When Mississippi Industrial College opened its doors on Memphis Street that year, serving as treasurer of the board of trustees was James Holmes Teer. The Teer story was of course exceptional, but his brother-in-law Henry Freeman also accumulated a substantial holding on Coldwater, and several former slaves, including Allen Perkins, Mack Fennell, and Joe Oliver, now owned small farms along Mt. Pleasant Road near Strawberry Church. After a 1909 visit to Holly Springs, Booker T. Washington reported that when he "inquired of both white people and colored people why it was the two races were able to live on such friendly terms, both gave almost the same answer. They said that it was due to the fact that in Marshall County so large a number of colored farmers owned their own farms." That was probably true in Marshall, but most African Americans in Mississippi would continue to work land "on shares" for many decades.[5]

Back across Coldwater Bottom from the Holmes Teer place and down Mt. Pleasant Road past Mack store at Strawberry Plains, the century had begun with a sad event. While walking in the yard, Martha Greenlee Davis had a dizzy spell, fell, and broke her hip. The injury made her an invalid, but though often in pain, she responded to this turn of fate as she had to all the others, keeping her spirits up and never complaining. Her family and friends were attentive. For years Eliza Jane Stephenson, now Mrs. Taylor and twice the widow of wealthy men, drove out from Holly Springs every week to spend an afternoon with her valued friend. The Finley cousins kept in close touch, and her grandchildren were her joy. They wanted to hear about the house before the war, and once one asked her whether she felt any remorse about shooting that Yankee. "No," she said, "I felt as if I had killed a rattlesnake." They were also curious about their grandfather. All family pictures had been destroyed when the house was burned. Although her children had located a daguerreotype of their mother in Virginia and had it copied, no likeness of Col. Davis could be found, so she kept in her bedroom a portrait of Robert E. Lee, whom she thought her husband resembled. After six years of be-

Martha Greenlee Davis
in old age. Courtesy
of Mary Ann Stanback
Wilson

ing an invalid, on a cold January day of 1906, Martha Greenlee Davis died at Strawberry Plains at the age of eighty-three. The family was never able to afford to have her grave marked.[6]

They may well have considered it year after year, but more pressing concerns always interfered. Repeatedly the Davises borrowed small sums from George Finley to tide them over difficult periods. Barely weathering the hard times, Johnny Davis had managed to pay only the interest on his mortgaged land. Finally, in 1912, Johnny Davis realized that he would have to sacrifice the north 243 acres of the original plantation in order to pay his mortgage off on the homestead tract. He sold the north tract to the Finleys. Using that money, he arranged that, on the last day of 1912, the unencumbered title to the 397 acres in the southern half of Section 12 be transferred in equal shares to himself and his now-widowed sister Mary Davis Moseley. The tract represented less than half of the acreage that Strawberry Plains had covered at its peak before the war. It was a comfort to Johnny that he had kept the plantation from going out of the Greenlee family completely, but the Finleys now owned more of Strawberry Plains than those of Davis blood.[7]

For the next few years, Johnny Davis seemed to be getting his part of the family farm on a sound footing. He made some good crops, and in the fall, amid the acrid smell of the pecan grove, the gin was kept humming from dawn to dusk. Like everyone, he was fond of his sister Mary (whose husband had died in 1909), but he was particularly attached to his niece Martha Moseley, who had been born at Strawberry Plains and grown up there amid her extended family. One bond they shared was a love of horses. In 1912 Martha, now a girl of eighteen, met a new riding companion. Mrs. Lizzie Anderson Fant and her daughter Netty, an artist in her thirties who had trained at the Art Institute in Chicago and the Art Students League in New York, had moved out from Holly Springs to the Anderson plantation north of Mack. Happily occupied painting landscapes, Netty Fant was also a horsewoman, and soon she and Martha, on her horse Jessie, were riding together all over the countryside. Martha Moseley also made Strawberry Plains a welcoming place for all the Davis kin. In 2005, one of Ann Winifred Davis Stanback's granddaughters, then a charming lady of ninety-nine, remembered Strawberry Plains in her childhood as the "place I'd rather go than any place in the world." Her cousin Martha was her favorite there, "so hospitable and generous," and so ready to see that her little cousin had a good time.[8]

Mary Davis Moseley and her daughter, Martha, standing by the west wall of the reconstructed mansion circa 1910. Courtesy of Mary Ann Stanback Wilson

John Presley Davis standing by Jessie, the horse of his niece Martha Moseley. Courtesy of the Audubon Mississippi/Strawberry Plains Finley Collection, University of Mississippi

At the turn of the century, four miles to the southeast of Strawberry Plains, George Finley and his family were still living in the brick plantation cottage off the Ashland road that he had built at the time of his marriage. His wife, Nannie Dunlap, had brought a strain of what people at the time called "melancholia" into the Finley family. It would eventually have tragic consequences in two of their children, but there were no indications of things to come at the beginning of the century. There were four children—John Latta (b. 1872), George Thornwell (b. 1876), Emma (b. 1878), and Thomas (b. 1881). John was married and living in Grenada, Mississippi, where he was in the cotton business. He would later move to Memphis and join the Sledge and Norfleet Cotton Company as vice-president. George Thornwell was farming the Gibbons-Puryear-Finley place for his father and had formed a partnership with L. A. Rather in the Finley Lumber Company. Emma was living at home, and Thomas was a student at the University of Mississippi.[9]

In 1906, the elder George Finley moved his family into Holly Springs, where he purchased the Jones-Shuford house, a spacious two-story, columned antebellum structure on Falconer Street. Though he had never been active in politics, he was elected to the 1890 constitutional convention—a measure of the respect in which he was held in the county. His opinion was still sought on many matters. The family remained pillars of the Presbyterian church, and they enjoyed town life and proximity to numerous kin and a wide circle of friends. He read widely and made periodic trips to Hot Springs, Arkansas, for his health. The family had lived in town for only four years when George Finley died in October 1910. His obituary in the Holly Springs *South* mentioned his father's death when George was fourteen and noted that "he took his place as head of the family assuming responsibilities beyond his years. So excellent was his judgment, that he was always the advisor of his mother and sisters." Given that excellent judgment, it is surprising that, like his father, he left no will. Again a group of Finley heirs would own everything in a large estate in common, and one among them would be called upon for years of complicated administration.[10]

Cousin George Finley's death was felt both personally and financially at Strawberry Plains. For forty years, he had come to the aid of his aunt and cousins over and over again. But he had taught his children their family responsibilities. In 1912 when Johnny Davis needed to sell the northern part of Section 12, in order to regain an unencumbered title to the home tract, George Finley's heirs bought the Strawberry Plains land, just as their father would have done.

At Mr. Finley's death, the eldest son, John, was living in Memphis, and Thomas, the youngest, was a banker in Holly Springs. It was the second son, George Thornwell Finley, who succeeded his father as manager of the Finley farming operation, which included the McKissack plantation. Through a complicated series of developments, this middle tract of the Strawberry Plains Audubon Center would figure in Finley affairs for over a century. Mrs. Alexander McKissack died in 1900, leaving the place to her sister's son Percy Cauthorn, a bachelor who himself died in 1909. He died without a will, and his estate went even further from the McKissack bloodline to his four Cauthorn aunts and one uncle (or to their children). The land, still under Finley management, was now owned in undivided fifths by the Cauthorn heirs (that is, each heir owned a fifth of the whole, not a specified and identified number of acres). In the following two years, the Finleys purchased two of the undivided fifths, and under the shared Cauthorn-Finley ownership, George Thornwell Finley continued to manage the place with the same care and sense of fairness that his father had. In a statement to the Cauthorn heirs in 1911, he listed the accounts of the sharecroppers, and then offered this explanation: "Joe Greer's rent has been reduced because his land has washed so badly and become so worn that he was not able to pay rent and his store account. While we have nothing to do with his account, we do know that his rent has been practically all he made." Not only were the Finleys not the sort of people to exploit sharecroppers, but they were also willing to make adjustments to help their tenants survive economic hardships.[11]

In the ten years following his father's death, George Thornwell Finley was very successful, both in handing affairs of the estate and in consistently expanding his own ventures. His only sister, Emma, who had first showed distressing signs of unbalance in 1905, was now in a sanitarium in Cincinnati. With money always set aside for Emma, George ran the holdings of the estate under the name Finley Brothers. In addition, George's lumber company was a thriving business, and he was involved in a couple of separate planting partnerships and in buying land alone and with his brother Thomas. He had also established a solid portfolio of bonds and stocks, including shares in Firestone Tire, Goodyear Tire, and the Coca Cola Company. But despite his great material success, George also was experiencing terrible periods of depression. Toward the end of the decade, he was sent to an institution in Michigan that tried to effect a cure by intense physical labor in the open air. Though, at age forty, he hated the regimen, he came home apparently cured. But in the summer of 1921, he felt the darkness descend again. As was his custom, every day he would drive out in his 1918 Buick to the Gibbons-Puryear-Finley place to check on the progress of the crop. As a deeply worn path later bore witness, he would pace up and down along a bank of the Coldwater River tortured by his thoughts. On July 28, 1921, he made up his mind. After binding his hands together with neckties, he jumped into the stream and drowned.[12]

It was his youngest brother who was called to identify the body. Thomas Finley, father of the two sisters who bequeathed Strawberry Plain Audubon Center, was the last male Finley left in Marshall County. It was now his time to assume the family burdens and responsibilities.

13

SHARECROPPING IN THE DEPRESSION

SOON AFTER THOMAS FINLEY assumed management of the complicated Finley assets, he began the long, slow process of disentangling interests and consolidating and simplifying. Heirs still held in common some of the holdings of the estates of his grandparents John Tate and Mary Jane Greenlee Finley. Thomas and his brother and sister each had an undivided one-third interest in the estates of their parents George J. and Nannie Dunlap Finley and of their brother George Thornwell Finley, who had also died without a will. And there was an additional complication—each of the three siblings owned an undivided one-third interest in an undivided two-fifths of the McKissack plantation.[1]

In 1921 the Finley farming operation had twenty-one renters. Some of them were men who rented large tracts for which they paid fixed sums, but most of them were sharecroppers. The sharecropping system was used by virtually all landowners, both white and black, and most sharecroppers in Marshall County were African American. Economic historians marvel at the fact that a system forged out of the economic desperation following the Civil War remained in place in the South for nearly a century. Not only did the system perpetuate the existence of a predominantly black peonage, but it kept the entire region well behind the rest of the nation, which during the same period was experiencing phenomenal economic growth. No fundamental changes in the methods of producing cotton had been made in decades. The process was still hand labor with a hoe and a one-row tiller drawn by a mule. The landowner would provide a tract of land and a mule and advance funds as needed. At the end of the season, the tenant would have to pay back any money advanced and give the landowner the agreed-upon share (usually half) of the yield of cotton bales. The tenant could sell all of the seed separated from his cotton, in good years getting as much as fifty dollars. It was usually with that money that he paid back any indebtedness to the landowner and to storekeepers. The farm with which Thomas Finley was most directly involved was the Gibbons-Puryear-Finley place. It has been described by the daughter of a tenant as "a sharecropping farm," where her father "worked on half." She recalled, "Mr. Tom had a reputation as being a fair man. In the fall, he always gave his hands their fair half."[2]

Even as Thomas Finley worked toward achieving some coherence in Finley affairs, his cousins at Strawberry Plains found themselves in need of Finley help again. According to Martha Moseley, her uncle John Davis had Strawberry Plains running on a sound basis through the end of World War I. In the autumn of 1918, however, he fell in the gin and broke his leg, and the next year a plummeting cotton market ruined Davis and many other farmers who delayed selling their cotton, hoping for an upturn in the market that never came. In the succeeding lean years, he tried to regain his losses, but declining health handicapped his efforts. Finally, with death approaching, he knew that he had to sell what was left of the plantation in order to provide for his niece. In January 1927, John P. Davis and his niece (as the only heir of her mother, who had died in 1919) sold the last 397 acres of Strawberry Plains held by the Davises to Thomas Finley for $5750. A month later, Thomas purchased from his brother John Latta Finley his undivided one-third interest in all the Finley land in Marshall County, including the remainder of the Strawberry Plains acreage on Section 12. Two years afterward, Thomas Finley bought from the heirs of his aunt Betsy Hull Finley the other half section of the Davis plantation on Section 7 that her husband had purchased in 1868. By 1930 Thomas had reunited the entire 960-acre expanse that Strawberry Plains had covered before the Civil War.[3]

Finleys now owned Strawberry Plains, but provisions had been made for the last of the Davis heirs. Though not stated in the deed, it was understood that Martha Moseley would have a lifetime tenancy in the house and be allowed to rent a small portion of the land. She felt a fierce devotion to the old place. She had turned down one offer of marriage from a Moseley cousin in Texas because she would not desert Uncle Johnny and the beloved place her people had carved

The stark old mansion at Strawberry Plains looms behind its avenue of cedars in the twentieth century. McAlexander Collection

from the wilderness. She held on the best way she could, and, by continuing to live in the ruined house for the next forty years, she saved it from destruction. She rented about thirty acres, enough acreage for her to have two sharecroppers. The boll weevil had already infested the South, which entered the Great Depression long before the rest of the country did. Living conditions in the great shell of the Davis mansion would never get better. Electricity and running water would never be added. Woodwork would never be painted. In the 1960s, the parlor presented merely a much worn version of the way it had looked in 1867.[4]

Martha Moseley (1894–1986) as a young woman. Courtesy of the Audubon Mississippi/Strawberry Plains Finley Collection, University of Mississippi

On November 24, 1927, John Presley Davis died. His obituary commented on the family's early settlement of the region and their prominence. Among his pallbearers was Euclid Woodfin McAlexander, Martha's old schoolmate at Mack School. Shy and reticent, Euclid had served along with two of his brothers in World War I, had been gassed in France, and suffered from a weakened constitution. In 1920 he had moved from Mack over to the old mansion at Strawberry Plains to help John Davis in running the plantation. He was a godsend in the invalid's last days. Afterward, he remained in the house helping Martha to care for her remaining invalid uncle, the demanding and ungrateful Uncle Eben. The 1930 census lists Euclid as "lodger." By 1935 when the bitter old man died at age eighty-eight, Euclid had become a fixed presence at Strawberry Plains, and he continued to live there with Martha until his death in 1957. Having worked for a time as a salesman, Euclid had an automobile, but because of his health, the state of the country roads, and the economic climate, Euclid and Martha lived an isolated existence. Euclid must have been in love with her (it is said that he carried her picture throughout the war), and clearly she loved him too—but like a brother. Her Stanback cousins considered him a member of the family. Martha would say that, after her uncle Johnny's death in 1927, she did not experience a similar loss until Euclid's death thirty years later. She gave a lonely, sensitive, sickly man a home, and he provided her companionship over long, difficult years. Of course there was talk, but Martha Moseley, so gentle and ladylike, had set her own course and looked neither to the left nor the right. She was not an unconventional person, but these were exceptionally hard times, and she had to live by her own lights. Martha Moseley is as much the heroine of Strawberry Plains as her grandmother Martha Trimble Greenlee Davis and as much the heir of Mary McDowell Greenlee, the iconic pioneer of the Valley of Virginia.[5]

An agricultural historian wrote of the state's "severe economic depression for two decades beginning in 1920," but bad times became worse following the stock market crash in 1929. Strawberry Plains sharecropper Zeek Stephenson would recall that 1933 was the hardest of all the years. The Finley farming ledgers show six Finley sharecroppers working at Strawberry Plains that year—Emmet Rankin, Ollie Mathis, Zeek Stephenson, Zeek Stephenson Jr., and Tom Jeffries. Also living on the place were Martha Moseley's two sharecroppers, Buck Harris and Felix Oliver.[6]

In 1933 Zeek Stephenson was sixty-eight. A granddaughter describes her mulatto grandfather as a "short, bowleg white man" and his wife as "a tall, skinny, jet-black woman." In 1884 Zeek had married Martha Jane Bates, called "Pinky," who had been raised on Strawberry Plains. After their marriage they settled there as sharecroppers. Zeek, who also worked in the Davis cotton gin, lost an arm in a ginning accident. It must have been strange to live in such proximity to the man he knew was his father, the remote and bad-tempered Eben Davis Jr. Today no one can tell us how they interacted. Zeek lived on the place until his wife's death in 1942. Both he and his wife are buried in Mack Cemetery, along with other Stephenson slaves and their descendants.[7]

Martha Jane's grave is marked, but Zeek's is not, as is the case with most of the African American graves in what began as slave burying grounds on the three converging plantations on Mt. Pleasant

Henry Stephenson Jr. (1891–1920), photographed while serving as a private in the 157th Depot Brigade during World War I. Henry grew up on Strawberry Plains and was the brother of Zeek Stephenson Jr. (1888–1950s) and son of Zeek Stephenson (1865–1945), both sharecroppers on Strawberry Plains. Courtesy of Willie Hayes Mallory

Road. Of the three, the slave-sharecropper cemetery at Strawberry Plains was the least accessible. It is located on the high ridge across the ravine from the big house and near the ruins of the slave quarters, a logical enough placement during the time when those to be buried lived on the ridge. Only two tombstones stand today, though rock markers and depressions in the earth indicate more than a score of graves. Certainly the loyal Davis servants and later valued sharecroppers Uncle Frank and Aunt Margaret Lee were buried there in the early 1900s. Probably also lying there are members of the Hunt

Felce Oliver (1927–2000), son of Felix Oliver Jr. (1908–1971), the bluesman, church singer, and deacon, who was a sharecropper on Strawberry Plains. Felce Oliver was a valued employee of Martha Moseley during her last years. His great-grandfather was a founding deacon of Strawberry Plains Missionary Church. Courtesy of Willie Hayes Mallory

family, slaves on Strawberry Plains, descendants of Nelson Hunt, born in 1818 in North Carolina. By the 1930s, the dirt road leading from the graveled Mt. Pleasant Road into Strawberry Plains was hazardous much of the year for both automobiles and wagons. There was no bridge over the deep-channeled branch that lay between the public road and the house, and a vehicle had to go down a high bank, across a sand ditch (or in wet weather a small stream), and then climb the opposite bank. Even once that problem was surmounted, getting a wagon loaded with a coffin up the rough trail to the burial ground on the high ridge was even more treacherous. The last person interred in the old graveyard was Hilton Marr, stepson of Ernest Perkins, one of the African American landowners on Mt. Pleasant Road. Marr died in the early 1930s.[8]

Among the other families who probably were buried there in an earlier day were former slaves Henry and Minerva Harris, who were living on the plantation at the time of the first census after emancipation. In 1933 their son Henry (known as Buck) and his family were Martha Moseley's sharecroppers. They lived across the ravine from the big house in the old quarters, and Buck's wife, Ruby, was Martha Moseley's cook. The other Moseley sharecropper, Felix Oliver, was the grandson of Joe and Leatha Stephenson Oliver, substantial citizens of the community. Joe Oliver was one of the early freedman landowners, and his family lived on their own farm for forty years. During the 1920s, it was mortgaged to assist one of the Oliver kin, and in 1928 the white man holding the note demanded full payment. The Olivers lost their homestead. Family members found work where they could, the grandson Felix coming to Strawberry Plains as a sharecropper. In 1933 Felix and his family were living in a frame tenant house down the lane east of the big house. The Oliver connection with the place lasted fifty years.[9]

The importance of Felix Oliver's house as a gathering for neighborhood blues musicians is the subject of one of the liveliest of the interviews done in the recently completed Strawberry Plains Oral History Project. Grace Mallory Turner, born in 1918, recalled going to Felix's house several times with her father, King Mallory, a talented local musician, when he, Felix, and a man named Jim Shipp gathered to play tunes like "Uncle Ned." Mallory was skilled at playing both the guitar and the fiddle, and Jim Shipp and Felix Oliver would "second him" on the guitar, while a group of neighbors danced to the blues music into the early morning hours. "I went on the floor around nine o'clock," Grace Turner told the interviewer. "When I got off the floor, it was near two o'clock. When I got off the floor, I said, 'Lord, I'll never do that again.'" Grace Mallory married soon after these visits to the Oliver place, and the sessions at Felix Oliver's house ceased about the same time. Perhaps the music and laughter were too loud, or perhaps this was about the time that Felix became more active in singing at Strawberry Church, which disapproved of such gatherings, even when no liquor was drunk as it was in the juke joints.[10]

But while they lasted, the sessions at Felix's house were an important diversion in the midst of the Great Depression, when for pleasure the sharecroppers mainly had to depend upon the simple pastimes of their ancestors, like fishing and hunting, which also supplemented their basic fare. Though sharecropping during the period was often a hard-scrabble existence, the tenant families on Strawberry Plains never lacked nourishment. According to Buck Harris's daughter, they raised hogs, cows, and chickens, and each family had a "garden patch," where they grew cabbage, tomatoes, onions, greens,

beans, English peas, okra, squash, and potatoes—both sweet potatoes and Irish potatoes. There was also plenty of molasses, made
from the sorghum grown on the place. Zeek Stephenson's niece recalls wanting to visit because her aunt "*always* had that big old pot of
peas and that *great*, big, old ham bone in that pot," and always "some
kind of pudding or something or other to go along with it." Looking back, she realizes, "It wasn't no fancy-eating kind of meal, and
they going to have plenty of milk and butter on the table." Only on
an occasional Sunday would chicken and biscuits be served. To this
basic diet were added bass and catfish caught in ponds or in the Coldwater and wild game—squirrel, rabbit, and opossum.[11]

Children had to find their own amusements. The Oral History
Project interviews speak of only very basic homemade toys, like balls
and bats and rag dolls. Remembered with particular pleasure was the
joy of playing in the sand ditch (or branch) after a rain and building
frog houses. An Oliver child recalled her father, Willie Oliver, parch-
ing peanuts and using them for a guessing contest: "That was our
night game at home," she said. "We would be sitting around the fire.
And then he'd probably read something or other to us, some kind of
little book that he had."[12]

Willie Oliver had learned to read at Strawberry School, where his
children were now enrolled from Thanksgiving (after cotton picking)
to spring (before planting) and where his sister Savannah Oliver was
teaching. More was taught than reading, writing, and arithmetic, as
Monroe Howell (born 1919) reminisced: "I remember when I got a
whipping in school for playing marbles. Miz. Sweetie B. Bell caught
me. She said playing marble was the first step toward becoming a
gambler. When she finished with me, she had taught me that I didn't
want to become a gambler." Deportment was also taught at both the
school and the church, where Buck Harris was an usher. "You better
not be chewing gum," many a child learned. "He would walk up to
you and say, 'Spit it out!'"[13]

The church, more even than the school, was the heart of the neighborhood. Without any musical instrument until 1955, the church would
be filled during services by beautiful voices unaccompanied. The singing was lead by setting notes—a member would pitch the note, and
then all would follow, while at the same time patting their feet to
the rhythm. Of a number of powerful singers, the most memorable

Strawberry School, built in 1892. Courtesy of Willie Hayes Mallory

Interior of the Strawberry School. Courtesy of Willie Hayes Mallory

was Milledge Tabor. The son of a Stephenson slave and a noted midwife and named for Maj. Stephenson, he was a rock upon which the church rested, deacon and church clerk for forty years. No one who heard him sing could ever forget him. Rijane Freeman captures the experience perhaps most vividly in her church interview: "Mr. Milledge, that scound could sing, you hear me! You could hear him far and near! He just flap the big foots down, that man could really sing." Another member recalls, "You could hear them singing before you got to church. You couldn't hardly wait to get there. Mr. Milledge would give out the hymn. He would give out the hymn and everybody would follow behind him." He frequently sang "Free at Last, Free at Last, Thank God All Mighty, I'm Free at Last." But his favorite song and that remembered by all members was actually a repeated verse from an Isaac Watt hymn, "When I Can Read My Title Clear":

When I can read my title clear to mansions in the skies,
I bid farewell to every fear and wipe my weeping eyes,
And wipe my weeping eyes, and wipe my weeping eyes.
I bid farewell to every fear and wipe my weeping eyes.

Should earth against my soul engage, and hellish darts be hurled,
Then I can smile at Satan's rage, and face the frowning world
And face a frowning world, and face a frowning world.
Then I can smile at Satan's rage, and face a frowning world.

Let cares, like a wild deluge come, and storms of sorrow fall,
May I but safely reach my home, my God, my heav'n, my All,
My god, my heav'n, my All, my God, my heav'n, my all.
May I but safely reach my home, my god, my heav'n, my All.

There shall I bathe my weary soul in seas of heav'nly rest,
And not a wave of trouble roll across my peaceful breast,
Across my peaceful breast, across my peaceful breast,
And not a wave of trouble roll, across my peaceful breast.

What better expression, sung in the rich, deep voice of Milledge Tabor, of the faith and hopes of these freedmen and their children.[14]

On the easternmost tract of Strawberry Plains Audubon Center, the Gibbons-Puryear-Finley place, stood another African American Baptist church, Finley Grove, with a school nearby. No one now knows just how old the first church building, a log structure, was. But it was an old church when Thomas Finley took over the farming operation in 1921, and he made a verbal promise that the land on which it stood belonged to the congregation as long as the organization continued. Not until 1976 was it necessary, for legal reasons, for the Finleys to give a formal Deed of Gift.[15]

These paired churches and schools, located at the western and eastern boundaries of the Audubon Center tract, sustained the African American community through the Great Depression and beyond. But that community had also witnessed what economic historians Ransom and Sutch have called "one of the largest migrations in human history." Nearly fifteen percent of the black population left the cotton-growing South between 1910 and 1940 and moved north seeking a better life. By the beginning of World War II, virtually every family had members living in St. Louis, Chicago, Detroit, and other northern cities. The schools and churches showed the effects. Strawberry School enrollment fell from 558 students in 1920 to 109 in 1937, and the membership of Strawberry Plains Missionary Baptist Church declined by half. A system of agricultural production and a way of life were still in place, but their days were numbered.[16]

14

A FAMILY'S VALUES

OVER THE SEVENTY-YEAR span that the Finleys owned Strawberry Plains and the adjoining lands, the region's agricultural economy changed dramatically. After World War II, as mechanization of agricultural production and large-scale irrigation of crops developed, King Cotton began to move west. Although the larger forces of agricultural economics would determine that the Strawberry Plains lands had no bright, remunerative future in cotton production, family history and family values were the deciding influences in what use would to be made of the tract in the twenty-first century.

Thomas Finley was forty in 1921, when he assumed management of the Finley assets in Marshall County after his brother George's death, and he was nearly fifty when he completed the purchase of all the Strawberry Plains acreage. He was a mature man, married with two daughters who would inherit a large estate. Just as he had been shaped by the joining of Finley and Dunlap strains, so his daughters would be both their father's and their mother's daughters. On October 7, 1907, in a large wedding at the Holly Springs Methodist Church, Thomas Finley married Ruth Leach. Of this union were born the benefactors of Strawberry Plains, Ruth in 1911 and Margaret in 1915. Their mother, Ruth Leach Finley, was an heiress and an orphan. Her father, Josuha Gilbert Leach, had joined the Confederate Army when only a boy and served during the whole four years of the conflict. In 1869 he moved from LaGrange, Tennessee, down to Holly Springs. "He started in here," his obituary noted, "without friends or capital, and built his career with his own good judgment and pluck, and without outside help amassed a considerable estate." As a contemporary descendant has put it, "Everything he touched turned to gold." In the 1880s, he established J. G. Leach, Stoves, Tinware, Hardware on the eastern side of the Holly Springs square. In 1898 he was a founder of Leach, McNamee Land and Timber Company in Mississippi County, Arkansas, at the town of Leachville. A year later, he was a founding director of the Merchants and Farmers Bank in Holly Springs (of which he was later president), and shortly thereafter a founding partner of the Holly Springs Stoneware Company. His first wife, Maria Butt, a local girl whom he married in 1878, died in 1894. Three years later, he took a second wife, a widow who had moved to town to teach music at North Mississippi Presbyterian College. At his death in 1904, he left four daughters by his first marriage and one by his second. The town historian would later comment that his was the "only estate I ever knew the public to underestimate." The story in my youth was that each of the five daughters had inherited twenty-five thousand dollars.[1]

The daughters, who were very close, had also quite distinct, independent personalities. Some of that independence, a descendant has suggested, came from the fact that each always had her own money. Ruth Leach was born in 1886, and during her mother's final illness she was taken to the home of her aunt Anna Parham Leach ("Nanna"), who became a much-beloved figure in her life and for whom she named her first daughter, Ruth Anna Finley. Ruth Leach had two older sisters. Mary, who was tubercular, had married and been taken to California for her health. She died in 1911. Cordelia Leach, who was the beauty of the family and who lifelong filled the role of older sister, married Lester Fant, a lawyer and scion of an old Marshall County family. In 1927 she purchased and carefully directed the restoration of the Clapp-West house, one of the finest Greek Revival mansions in Mississippi, and a general inspiration for Margaret Finley Shackelford's work on the Davis house at Strawberry Plains. The one younger full-sister was Margaret Leach, the most adventurous of the daughters. After graduating from college in Virginia and earning a master's degree in social work from Columbia University, Margaret took a grand tour of Europe, returning just as World War I was beginning. She worked for the Red Cross in flood relief during the twenties, for the YWCA, and was the mentor of early social workers in Mississippi. In 1938 Margaret built a summer home in the moun-

Thomas Finley (1881–1967) as a young man at Dawson Springs, Kentucky. Courtesy of National Audubon Society, Strawberry Plains Audubon Center

tains at Little Switzerland, North Carolina, and opened a gift shop in Holly Springs, where she did custom framing and sold mountain arts and crafts. After World War II, she was involved with the relocation of displaced persons from Europe. Pauline Leach Hammond, the younger half-sister, was a much-valued teacher in the Holly Springs public school.[2]

One influence that united all the Leach sisters was a basic, unpretentious (and tee-totaling) Methodism. Mr. Leach's obituary noted that he was a "consistent and devoted member of the Methodist church and for many years had been one of the Board of Stewards of the church at this place. He was public spirited, honorable, and upright." All his daughters remained lifelong Methodists, Ruth Leach refusing to go over to the strong Finley-Dunlap Presbyterian tradition, and Thomas Finley refusing to leave it.[3]

It was one of the few matters on which they could not agree. Otherwise they complemented each other well. With the sunniest disposition of all the Leach sisters, Ruth was positive, optimistic, and centered in the here-and-now, and she was a good balance to the

Ruth Leach Finley holding her firstborn, Ruth Anna Finley, in 1911. Courtesy of National Audubon Society, Strawberry Plains Audubon Center

tendency toward melancholy that Thomas Finley was heir to. Both liked to travel and found much pleasure in the natural world. Like his father, Thomas worked closely, particularly on conservation projects, with the local Mississippi Agricultural Experiment Station branch, headed then by Charles Tilton Ames. Ames was a fellow Presbyterian elder; and in 1928 Thomas Finley agreed to sell a portion of the Gibbons-Puryear-Finley place to the state for an expansion of the experiment station in Marshall County. Ruth Leach Finley was a birder, and many people recall her lifelong pleasure in observing the many varieties of birds in the region.[4]

After their wedding trip, the Finleys set up housekeeping in a small apartment on Market Street off the town square. Upon Thomas's father's death in 1910, they moved into the antebellum Finley house on Falconer Street, where Thomas's brother George Thornwell Finley was also living. Eventually they added a two-story wing to the back of the house, the upper floor taken up by a sleeping porch (a mark of all the houses of the Leach sisters), and the lower floor by a screened porch, which Ruth surrounded with bird feeders. Each Monday, she

Ruth and Margaret Finley dressed as moth and butterfly. Courtesy of
the Strawberry Plains Audubon Center

and her sister Cordelia Leach Fant had their cooks bake a week's supply of cornbread to feed the birds.[5]

The Finley daughters, Ruth Anna and Margaret, who attended the
Methodist church with their mother, had a happy, secure home life.
One important influence that Margaret would recall was the wonderful books about nature that they had as children. Friends remembered the prize vegetable garden that Thomas Finley cultivated east of
the house and the excursions he took the children on to the farm on
Coldwater. In summers the family would travel in their large, open-
air Franklin automobile to the Mississippi gulf coast, up through Virginia to Washington, D.C., or to Monteagle, Tennessee, or later, to
Little Switzerland—stopping along the way for picnics.[6]

The Leaches shared the frugality of the Finleys. The Thomas Finleys lived comfortably, but, as one friend remarked with considered understatement, "they saved where they could." While no money was wasted and there was never any display, they provided their daughters with every advantage. On her sixteenth birthday in 1931, Margaret was given a grand piano (which today is in the parlor at Strawberry Plains). Both girls were sent to good schools. After a year at the local college, Ruth and a friend went to Randolph-Macon Women's College in Virginia for a year. She then spent a year at the University of Missouri studying journalism and finished at the University of Mississippi. Margaret also transferred a couple of times. She started at Belhaven College (a Presbyterian school for women in Jackson), then attended Ole Miss, and finished at the University of North Carolina at Chapel Hill, where she majored in sociology, perhaps influenced by her aunt Margaret Leach.[7]

After college, Ruth returned home to work as a bookkeeper at the Merchants and Farmer's Bank, where her father was then a director and eventually vice-president. After a few years, she quit to assist her father, to whom she was deeply devoted, with the bookkeeping for the Finley interests. In contrast, Margaret was focused upon a career. After graduate work in public administration at Chapel Hill, she spent a year working in Holly Springs in the Marshall County Health Department, before moving to Oklahoma and taking a position with the Oklahoma State Department of Health. In a 1945 wedding at the Finley home in Holly Springs, she married Dr. John W. Shackelford, who was also working in public health in Oklahoma. Thirteen years older, tall, lean, and very straight, he too was a Mississippian, from Carrollton, a graduate of Tulane Medical School and the Harvard School of Public Health. Both became leaders in their fields, he as head of the Oklahoma agency and she as state director of statistics.[8]

Ruth Anna Finley was active socially in Holly Springs, a member of the Holly Springs Garden Club and of the Thursday Club (the ladies literary club), and an avid bridge player. In 1947 she and her neighbor Mae Sage Hill were the first townspeople to tour Europe after the war. Ruth had an artistic side, and she purchased a magnificent Empire lamp in Paris to add to the period pieces she was col-

A 1947 passport photo of Ruth Anna Finley (1911–1984). Courtesy of National Audubon Society, Strawberry Plains Audubon Center

John and Margaret Finley Shackelford (1915–1998) in the late 1940s. Courtesy of National Audubon Society, Strawberry Plains Audubon Center

lecting for the Finley house to replace her mother's favored mission oak. She redecorated the place a couple of times, each time frugally hanging wallpaper herself. She was also appreciative of the natural world. Roxie Holloway, who worked in the Thomas Finley home, remembers well the Sunday afternoon that Ruth and her father embarked on an outing to bring back a native azalea from out on Spring Creek, where the Finleys had first settled. It was planted in view of the breakfast room window, where it can still be enjoyed. Ruth Finley was also an enthusiastic member of the National Trust for Historic Preservation.[9]

A few years after their marriage, Margaret and John Shackelford took on a project in Oklahoma City that foreshadowed in many ways what they would later do in Marshall County. In 1948 they purchased an overgrown, rough, uneven lot outside the city with a deep gully that strong rains would flood. After clearing the underbrush themselves, they built a house and then two years later fulfilled a dream (carefully prepared for and researched on trips to New England) of constructing a two-room stone mill house with a working water wheel. Water from a pool surrounded by a spacious terrace was recirculated through the trace. All the stonework they did themselves, and John Shackelford took pride in constructing a large retaining wall. When interviewed by the Oklahoma City newspaper for an article on the house, the Shackelfords pointed out that the place was a refuge for birds, "robins, redbirds, mocking birds, thrushes, thrashers, woodpeckers, flickers, chickadees and summer and winter—wrens." John was becoming a devoted naturalist, and Ruth Leach Finley made him a present of a membership in the Audubon Society.[10]

Mrs. Finley's serious interest in birds continued growing over time. She was clear in her disapproval of bird hunting, and she did what she could to stop town boys from killing birds with their pellet guns— having groups of them to her house and plying them with cokes and cookies while reasoning with them about the value and beauty of the species. The town was to remember most, however, how she doted on her pet parakeet. He had the run of the Finley house, even though lady visitors were clearly apprehensive about his landing on their heads or hats. But she loved the bird, which she had taught to say his name and the Finley telephone number, "Chuckles Finley, 63."

The Finley house. Drawing by H. Rather from *Out of the Skillet: Old
Southern Recipes*, St. Anne's Guild of the Parish of Christ Church,
Holly Springs, Mississippi (1947)

On a visit home, forgetting the freedom Chuckles enjoyed, Margaret
Shackelford left a door ajar, and the bird escaped. For the next several days, though the bird would come back to the yard and perch in
trees, attempts to lure him back into the house all failed. Finally the
day came when he did not return, and he was never seen again. But
Chuckles had entered local folklore.[11]

By the late 1950s, sweeping changes were being felt in the cotton-
growing South. Propelled by mechanization and the growing use of
insecticides, a revolution in the Mississippi cotton economy began
after World War II. "A two-row cotton picker," noted Mississippi
agricultural historian William Lincoln Giles, "will harvest more in
a day than 140 field hands," and a tractor "will do more work in
a day and do it better than several dozen mules with drivers." The
growing use of machinery would spell the end of the sharecropping
system. The first phase of what has been called the Great Migration
of African Americans from the South, beginning with World War
I, was driven by the promise of economic and social opportunity in

Finley sharecropper and mule in the 1940s. Courtesy of the Audubon Mississippi/Strawberry Plains Finley Collection, University of Mississippi

the North. As a scholar of the Southern Diaspora has written, the second exodus following World War II came after "mechanical cotton pickers destroyed what was left of the rural black economy." The first mechanical pickers were used in Marshall County in 1952—interestingly enough, in fact, in Coldwater Bottom. An agricultural authority stated that by 1970 cotton was produced in Mississippi with no hand labor.[12]

But during the 1950s, most cotton in Marshall was still picked by hand and planted and cultivated by men and mules. On Saturdays from shortly after noon until long after dark, the Holly Springs square was still filled with black sharecroppers come to town to buy supplies and to visit friends from all over the county. Every afternoon during the week, it was still a familiar sight to see Thomas Finley leaving the Merchants and Farmers Bank in his farm clothes. He would get into his old coupe and stop at Booker's Hardware on the square for gas, always cautioning the attendant not to overfill the tank. He would then head out Highway 7 to the Gibbons-Puryear-Finley place on Coldwater. Then in his seventies, he was still farming the old way, reluctant to displace either man or beast. His black sharecroppers remained as long as they wished and continued to farm with mules. The large mule barn on the place stood until the last of his stock had died. Finley was also a familiar presence in the Presbyterian church, where he was an elder and continued to assist with communion into his eighties, an increasingly feeble but distinguished gentleman.[13]

Thomas Finley was very much a conservator, and over the decades of his stewardship the Finley assets steadily grew. By the end of the twentieth century, they would be valued in the millions of dollars. He operated conservatively, however, in a way that few people in the contemporary world would understand. He never, for example, raised the rent on a tenant. Once he was satisfied with a tenant, that man was assured that he would always have the land at the same rate, no matter what other offers Finley received. "I never heard anybody say a bad word against him," commented Boe McClure, who rented the Gibbons-Puryear-Finley place for twenty years after Thomas Finley gave up farming. After his daughter Ruth had assumed management of the Finley assets, one group of heirs of the McKissack plantation, which the Finleys had been running for seventy years, offered to sell their portion to the Finley family. When the sale was final, R. A. McPherson wrote: "In all of the years of association with your father and you, I have never had a cause to make a complaint and in the years ahead I will feel a bit nostalgic for not having communication with such fine people."[14]

Thomas and Ruth Leach Finley died within months of each other in 1967, leaving wills bequeathing everything to Ruth Finley and Margaret Finley Shackelford in undivided halves. By that time, the daughters were already forming plans for the large estate they inherited, and in particular for the Finley land north of Holly Springs. In 1968 Margaret Shackelford wrote a letter of inquiry to the National Wildlife Foundation: "My sister and I own a tract of land in north central Mississippi which we would like in some way to dedicate permanently as a sanctuary for God's creatures other than man. We are interested in finding a perpetual organization which can accept land as a gift and maintain it for [a] wildlife sanctuary in a manner to be agreed upon in some kind of trust arrangement. The tract is approximately three square miles in size. Some of it is under cultivation, some in pasture and woods, a small part is a swampy area." It would be fifteen years before the sisters settled upon the organization to which they would leave the land, but already they knew what they wanted to do. They would memorialize both their parents in a manner that perpetuated the values of both.[15]

Ruth Finley continued the management of the estate as she had done for the last years of her father's life. Boe McClure speaks of her reluctance to permit any hunting on the Finley land he rented or to allow the cutting of as much as a single tree. Her decision in the late 1960s not to disturb recently built beaver dams laid the groundwork for what is now the state's largest beaver colony and dam.[16]

At the time of the Finleys' deaths, Dr. John Shackelford was sixty-five and facing retirement, and Margaret herself would soon have accumulated thirty years service in public health. Considering the needs of her sister, her husband, and herself, Margaret began to think about returning to Mississippi. Ten years earlier, as a college freshman, I had written for the local newspaper an essay on Strawberry Plains that captured her interest (Margaret had been the only attendant in my mother's wedding in 1937). Although Martha Moseley, the poor country cousin, had monthly visited the Finley home in town, Margaret had never been out to the stark and decaying old brick mansion in the country. She and John now visited it, were captivated, and began to think about the rehabilitating the now abandoned place. Ruth was alone and needed nearby companions. John would require projects to engage his energies, and both he and Margaret would love country living. They decided that they would retire to Strawberry Plains and revitalize the old mansion.

Martha Moseley had continued to live out at Strawberry Plains for several years after Euclid McAlexander's death in 1957, with only her large shepherd-mix dog, Sandy, as companion. The gentle and dependable Ollie Mathis lived in the three-room tenant house within sight of the brick house to the west, and Felix Oliver still occupied the house just down a lane to the east. Ollie was too old to farm, but Felix was still sharecropping. Their proximity gave Martha some sense of security. Few visitors drove down the badly washed and treacherously rutted old road to see her, and in wet winter weather, one would have to park a car along the first field after the church and walk over the rickety bridge and up the deeply sunken ancient road to the house. But in the afternoons, she was always dressed to see guests—invariably in a skirt, blouse, and cardigan (if needed) and wearing cotton stockings and sensible shoes. One was always taken through the rough cavernous hall into the worn parlor. Refreshment was never offered, but the welcome was warm, and she would occasionally slip out into what was apparently an adjoining back bedroom to bring back an old photograph or a timeworn document. I remember many a darkening afternoon spent in that parlor, lighted only by a coal oil lamp, listening (sometimes still bundled in an overcoat) to her, as she sat on a footstool by the open fire and recalled the history of the place and of the neighborhood.[17]

In 1964, when she was seventy, Martha Moseley moved into town to live first in a small outbuilding owned by a close and caring cousin, Augusta Brittenum Greene, whose own once considerable fortune was now wiped out, and then later in another ramshackle building. As was the Finley way, although the Finleys had owned Strawberry Plains for forty years, Margaret Shackelford considerately and scrupulously kept Martha informed of all her plans for Strawberry Plains. It was wonderful for Martha Moseley to know in her old age that the place she loved above all else would be saved and treasured.

On August 3, 1971, Holly Springs architect Hugh H. Rather submitted to the Shackelfords the architectural drawings for the "restoration" of the old brick house. The plan was not actually a restoration, for there was no attempt to return the structure to its original 1851 vernacular Federal appearance. The sources of inspiration, instead, were the Greek Revival mansions of Holly Springs. John and Margaret subsequently sold their Oklahoma City property and moved into the tenant house that Ollie Mathis had occupied, living there during the years of work on the dilapidated and decaying old mansion. It was a huge undertaking, much of it a reconstruction, and one carpenter recalled Margaret's frequent admonition to the workers to remember that she and John were living on a fixed income.[18]

The Shackelfords were actively involved in overseeing the whole renovation. John was enjoying physical exercise, riding the mowing machine over the open lands surrounding the house, and supervising construction of a storage building and rustic retreat for entertaining to the east of the house. As the building was going on, the Shackelfords collected furnishings and fixtures for the house. Nineteenth-century marble mantles were found to go in the downstairs rooms, and Margaret and Ruth discovered in the old Shrine Club being razed in Memphis a magnificent colonial revival balcony stairway, which could be made to fit the hallway. Clarence Coleman, a skilled Marshall County carpenter, took down the staircase in Memphis and, following the plans of the Finley sisters, rebuilt and modified it to fit the house at Strawberry Plains. It stands as an impressive example of the recycling of historic materials. In the midst of work on the house, a disagreement arose that led to one of the memorable stories connected with Strawberry Plains. Dr. John Shackelford was pleased with the original architect's drawing, which called for a house covering only the footprint of the original brick structure. But Margaret gradually decided that she wanted a wing added to the back of the house, with a library, laundry room, and a wide enclosed porch-hallway, joining the original structure and connecting with a two-bay carport. She had her way. But in a gesture reflecting the kind of true Southern eccentricity not unknown historically in Marshall County, John, though relishing their other projects and their life at Strawberry Plains, would never enter the completed addition.[19]

In November 1974, a Holly Springs friend wrote me about an excursion on "one of those really rare and beautiful Indian Summer afternoons" to see the Shackelfords and the house: "John greeted us in the yard of the little house and we visited with him while Margaret and Ruth bid other visitors at the main house goodbye. After they returned, we learned that it was Martha and some of the Moseleys. I was sorry then that I hadn't gone over to speak. . . . About the time we said 'hello' to Margaret and Ruth, Maxine and C. C. drove up. We all went over to see the progress, which has been a lot since last I was there. The rear wing is almost completed and to my notion, makes the house far more attractive. . . . [We] went back to the east lawn of the little house for drinks. It was almost as warm as early summer and we stayed during a beautiful sunset until first dark." The account captures well the sense of ease and hospitality that characterized the place in its beautiful, peaceful setting during all the years of the Shackelford tenure.[20]

John and Margaret moved into the house the next spring. Martha Moseley had given them some of the original parlor furniture saved when the house was burned during the Civil War—a low Empire sofa, a mahogany card table, two side chairs, and a rocking chair, as well as the original walnut country Sheraton dining room table and a post-war plantation desk. Soon the John Latta Finley family in Memphis also brought to the house furniture from the early Finley family that included the baby bed that Mary Jane Greenlee Finley's children had slept in.[21]

Margaret Shackelford had planned well for beginning a productive new chapter upon their return to Mississippi. Reestablishing old bonds of friendship and cultivating new ones, she and Dr. Shackelford immediately became engaged in the life of town and county. They enjoyed sharing Strawberry Plains with other people and entertained often. Their retirement was a happy span of years. But shadows did come. In 1979, Ruth Finley was diagnosed with Parkinson's disease. It was now time to make final decisions about the disposition of the Finley properties. On January 19, 1983, local newspapers announced that the Finley house in town, the restored brick mansion at Strawberry Plains, and all the Finley lands north of Holly Springs were to be bequeathed to the National Audubon Society, supported by a substantial endowment.[22]

On March 24, 1984, Ruth Finley died, and little over a year and half later, on December 28, 1985, Dr. John Shackelford died of pancreatic cancer. With characteristic resiliency, Margaret carried on her life at Strawberry Plains. Within the next two weeks Martha Moseley died at age ninety-two in a nursing home; she had lived in Holly Springs for twenty-two years after leaving Strawberry Plains. Margaret saw to the arrangements and carried out final wishes that Martha's car be given to Felce Oliver (Felix Oliver's son), who had attended to her various small needs during the last years. Margaret had now outlived all the family involved in Strawberry Plains. After moving back to Mississippi, the Shackelfords had joined the Presbyterian church in Holly Springs, where Margaret's great-grandmother, Mary Jane Greenlee Finley, had been one of the earliest members and her own

The christening of Edward Stephenson McAlexander, the first social
occasion in the rehabilitated mansion at Strawberry Plains, August 24,
1975. On the far left, John and Margaret Finley Shackelford stand immediately to the right of the officiating minister. On the far right,
second from the end is Ruth Finley, seeking to avoid the camera as
she always did in her later years. Martha Moseley, wearing a long scarf,
stands sixth from the right. McAlexander Collection

father, Thomas Finley, had served as an elder for decades during
the twentieth century. Now, more than ever, she valued the "warm
family feeling" of the small congregation. She loved having people
out for bridge in her family room, where they could also watch the
birds and other wildlife. She was active in her clubs and had frequent
houseguests. She traveled with friends in Europe and the United
States and regularly went with groups to the theater and the sym-
phony in Memphis. In 1996 Margaret began discussions with the
Audubon Society about relinquishing her life share in Ruth's trust.
The society could then move into the Finley house in Holly Springs
as their headquarters and establish a presence at Strawberry Plains.
This was accomplished early in 1998, and she was pleased to see in

her lifetime the partial fruition of her careful plans. She died, at age eighty-three, on October 9, 1998, after suffering a stroke at her beloved country home.[23]

Margaret Finley Shackelford is another of the great ladies of Strawberry Plains. Without her vision, the old brick house would never have been given a new life, nor the future of the house and land assured. At her funeral, the Presbyterian minister spoke of her "quiet determination and careful resolve." She was a preservationist, a naturalist, and an environmentalist. Without descendants, she insured that Finley stewardship would benefit posterity.[24]

15

AUDUBON CENTER

THE FIRST TWO years after the death of Margaret Finley Shack-elford were a time of planning and preparation. Jesse Grantham, a veteran Audubon biologist and sanctuary manager who had come to Holly Springs before her death, was named executive director of Audubon Mississippi with headquarters in the Finley house. In his first news release, Grantham noted the two-fold environmental mission of the office: "the responsibility of the whole state," as well as the creation of the Marshall County educational center. The National Audubon Society board met in Holly Springs in March 1999, and members were charged with developing a comprehensive plan for one of the largest gifts ever made to Audubon.[1]

In a 1982 paper drawn up by Ruth Finley and Margaret Finley Shackelford expressing their basic intentions for "this proposed nature and conservation preserve" comes this paragraph: "It is our earnest wish and desire that the name 'Strawberry Plains' be incorporated in the name of the proposed facility, or preserve, and stronger still is our wish and desire that this preserve or facility be considered and identified as a memorial to our parents, Thomas and Ruth Leach Finley." The name that Martha Greenlee Davis had bestowed upon her home almost 150 years earlier would continue to cast its spell, and the conservationist and naturalist legacy of the Finley family would be memorialized on this landscape. The first issue of the magazine published by the state Audubon office announced the preparation of the Finley land for "use as a center for environmental education and activism." Early in 2001, Director Jesse Grantham gave this report: "The farm was called Strawberry Plains; now it is called Strawberry Plains Audubon Center. It will be managed as a showcase for the conservation of birds and their habitat. The cattle and row crops are gone. And nature is coming back quickly, with meadows and hedgerows for grasshopper sparrows, yellow-breasted chats, and other songbirds in the summer to LeConte's sparrows and other migrants in the winter. There is a rookery of 25 great blue heron pairs in the Coldwater River bottom lands." The Strawberry Plains Audubon Center was to be opened to the public in the spring of 2001.[2]

In preparation, a manager was hired and put in charge of transforming the tenant house west of the big house into a visitor's center and environmental education facility. The building, which workers estimated had been built about 1900, had been the home of Ollie Mathis during the last decades of Martha Moseley's tenure at Strawberry Plains. In the early 1970s, John and Margaret Shackelford had added electricity and running water, a kitchen and a bath to the original three-room structure, so that they could live there for a couple of years while the big house was being rehabilitated. Once that renovation was completed and they had moved in, they kept the old tenant house rented out either to a young single man or to a young couple. The manager and two staff members now went to work gutting the structure and reconfiguring it to create a meeting and exhibit area, a space for a gift shop, two classrooms or offices, a sizable kitchen, and rest rooms. Throughout, they used materials that had been collected by Dr. Shackelford or recycled from old buildings either at Strawberry Plains or on the Finley property in Holly Springs. When the structure was finished, it was named the John and Margaret Finley Shackelford Environmental Education Center. The three buildings to the east of the big house that John Shackelford had used for projects and entertaining were outfitted for the John Shackelford Field Laboratory, the center director's office, and a maintenance shop with shed for the storage of equipment.[3]

By the time Strawberry Plains Audubon Center opened, a number of projects and incentives had already been initiated. In the last months of Margaret Shackelford's life, the rather formal back garden at the juncture of the two-story and one-story portions of the big house was redesigned as a more naturalistic space incorporating native species, especially those attractive to birds. More such plantings were installed at the education center and at other spots to highlight the need to visitors of reducing exotic and often invasive nonnative

Davis House at Strawberry Plains Audubon Center. Courtesy of National Audubon Society, Strawberry Plains Audubon Center

species. A bluebird trail was laid out linking a series of nest boxes for eastern bluebirds.[4]

The Audubon Center had already been opened for field trips for school children, a meeting of the Mississippi Ornithological Society, the annual meeting of the Mississippi Bluebird Society, and meetings of northern Mississippi garden clubs. The Davis House at Strawberry Plains had been opened for both the Holly Springs Pilgrimage (the second oldest tour of historic houses in Mississippi) and a local Christmas tour. The University of Tennessee, Mississippi State University, and the University of Memphis were now involved in research projects at the center, using student interns. Efforts were underway to build a base of volunteers, especially among retired adults and youth groups like the Eagle Scouts. What was to become a signature event at the Audubon Center, the fall Hummingbird Migration Celebration, had gotten off to a modest start, drawing a group of seventy-five people. In the spring of 2001, thirty acres of grassland were part of a controlled burn conducted by the Mississippi Forestry Commission. This measure, which had been practiced by the Chickasaws to keep down underbrush, was now undertaken to restore welcoming wildlife habitats. Afterward, the fields were planted in wildflowers and seed-producing species. Special attention had been given to the large beaver colony that Ruth Finley had allowed to develop on the eastern side of the property. The winter 2001 report remarked that these "areas support waterfowl populations throughout the year and a heron rookery in the summer. Wood ducks are present and nesting boxes have been erected in the beaver ponds. We have no immediate plans to change the present conditions of the beaver ponds. They provide excellent habitat for breeding and wintering waterfowl like ringed-neck duck, shoveler, mallard, gadwall, pintail, wood duck, green-winged and blue-winged teal, heron species, anhinga, bitterns and passerine songbirds (tree swallow, prothonotary warblers, red-headed woodpecker)." A plan was drawn for trails to take visitors to the edge of these wetlands, where boardwalks would enable them to have a "firsthand experience in interior wetland ecology." In summary, the report noted: "This Center will be fundamentally different from nature centers of the past, which primarily focused on natural history identification. Strawberry Plains Audubon Center will be a place where visitors develop a personal relationship with nature and gain an understanding of the relationship between themselves and the natural world. One of the goals will be to drive home the message of the importance of the relationship between plants and animals and how the future of the planet depends on understanding and maintaining that healthy relationship." A start had been made.[5]

In the summer of 2002, Jesse Grantham left Mississippi to go to Audubon Texas in Corpus Christi, and in the fall Madge Lindsay was hired as vice-president and executive director of Audubon Mississippi and the director of Strawberry Plains Audubon Center. A graduate of Texas A&M University with a degree in recreation, parks, and tourism sciences, she had spent over ten years at Texas Parks and Wildlife, where she created the Great Texas Coastal Birding Trail, the first regional birding trail established in the United States, which spawned the creation of birding trails throughout the country. In 2002 she was named one of seven "Heroes for Birds" by *Birders World* magazine and was co-authoring a book on Texas hummingbirds. She had also grown up on a cotton farm in northern Alabama, where she had developed a sense of the history and culture of a similar landscape.

One of her first initiatives was securing the services of Dr. Steve Brewer, plant ecologist at the University of Mississippi, to do a study entitled "Ecological Restoration of Natural Fire Regimes in Oak-Hickory Communities" for the Land Stewardship Committee of Strawberry Plains Audubon Center. Drawing upon an 1841 survey of interior section lines of nine Marshall County townships, including four of the sections that make up the center, the researchers determined the "early-colonial upland tree species composition" of the land. The study found that post oak, black jack oak, and black oak had dominated the presettlement upland landscape of central Marshall County. In the well-drained flood plains grew hickory, black gum, mulberry, sassafras, and black and white walnut; and in the poorly drained portions, white oak, sweet gum, maples, elms, yellow poplar, beech, dogwood, ashes, holly, ironwood, and water oak. Because of farming practices and the abandonment of systematic controlled burning, the original ecosystem had been disturbed, or in the terms of the study, "degraded." The report recommended "a combination of top killing off-site trees [thereby also providing ideal habitat for cavity-nesting birds] and prescribed burning" to begin to restore the old oak-hickory forests of the tract. Brewer's recommendations were followed, and he and his students continue to work with the center on a hardwood regeneration project.[6]

This was the first in a series of surveys of the resources at the center. The new director was particularly interested in tying the historical and cultural background (which Ruth Finley and Margaret Finley Shackelford had wanted recognized and preserved) in with the natural and ecological features, in order to offer a multifaceted experience for the visitor. "Although our main mission here at the preserve is to connect people with nature," Madge Lindsay stated, "our land and people history is much too extensive to ignore and should be recorded before it is lost." Toward that end, the center's History Steering Committee was assembled for a first meeting on June 24, 2003. The members represented the Center for the Study of Southern Culture at the University of Mississippi, the University of Georgia, Special Collections at the University of Mississippi, Strawberry Plains Missionary Baptist Church, Shackelford Trust advisors, and local people with backgrounds in historic architecture and regional history. At the meeting it was announced that all the Strawberry Plains and Finley papers were being donated to the University of Mississippi to be preserved and catalogued as the Audubon Mississippi/Strawberry Plains Finley Collection. A grant from the Mississippi Humanities Council, along with a contribution from Strawberry Plains Audubon Center, was funding an oral history project, conducted by the Center for the Study of Southern Culture, concentrating on those familiar with the Finley family and the experience of living on this land. Another grant proposal was in process to support an archeological survey of the center lands. The director's plan was that all these resources would eventually be used for a written history.[7]

This was a particularly active period in the history of the center. All offices had been relocated from the Finley house in town to Strawberry Plains, and restoration of the Holly Springs structure, now called Audubon Finley Place, was underway to provide housing for the director as well as a refurbished historic house for community functions and tourism. An interpretive specialist and gardens and volunteer coordinator had been hired, and a commemorative garden was being added to the garden space at the back of the Davis House. Entered through a wooden propalea, designed by architect Chelius H. Carter, the garden was a memorial to the two sister benefactors. The program of planting native species was expanded at the center, and a butterfly garden was started at the local high school. To gain direct access to Highway 311, Margaret Shackelford in her last years had purchased eighteen adjoining acres of the old Stephenson plantation from McAlexander heirs. Now Audubon Mississippi was also arranging (through a complicated land swap) to get title to twenty acres of the old William Seal plantation adjoining the center on the south and providing additional highway frontage. That swap was going forward. At the same time, the outreach of Audubon Mississippi was being expanded, and marketing and development strategies for the center were in the planning stage.[8]

In the spring of 2003, the preliminary archeological survey was completed by a University of South Carolina archeologist; the project had been funded by the Mississippi Humanities Council under the administration of Dr. Phillip Ensley. The survey revealed remains of three slave houses on the ridge south of the Davis House, old foundations at the center office suggesting that it was the site of a carriage house or stable, evidence of seven tenant houses on a line running roughly slightly southeast to northwest of the big house, and signs of at least sixteen unmarked graves (as well as two marked ones) in the African American cemetery. At the same time, a scholar from Hampton University submitted his report on vernacular architecture, focusing on the tenant houses of the tract, most of which were beyond repair. In late fall 2003, two archeologists and a crew of graduate students from the University of Mississippi conducted the first of a series of geophysical surveys. Their final report found evidence of two or more unmarked burials along the left margin of the Davis family cemetery, confirmed unmarked grave sites at the African American cemetery, and discovered traces of the old cotton gin north of the center's offices.[9]

In June 2003, a full-time ecologist and land manager was hired, and the center developed a comprehensive land management plan for the 2500-acre preserve. The seventh annual Forestry Field Day of the Marshall County Forestry Association, held at the center in October 2003, initiated an outreach program using the tract as a demonstration site for landowners in habitat management practices. Wagons transported the participants to four stops on the tract for observation of woodland, grassland, converted agricultural land, and the native landscape areas on the central campus. Among the speakers at the event was Dr. Steve Brewer, responsible for the report on ecological restoration for Strawberry Plains Audubon Center. The oral history project was well underway by January 2004 under the guidance of the director of documentation at the Center for the Study of Southern Culture, and the following June the Audubon Center held a workshop to survey progress and establish goals, "placing ecological conservation as the highest priority, followed by education and cultural heritage." The interviews with former sharecroppers and older members of the community were complete by fall, and on October 16, Strawberry Plains Audubon Center held a humanities workshop in Holly Springs to present to the public the results of the archaeological and cultural history projects.[10]

A director of education had been hired, and Madge Lindsay commented that "the education initiative with youth and adults will expand and help Strawberry Plains spread its wings." Soon bimonthly classes were being offered to the general public, student ecology exhibits were announced, and in June 2004 the center hosted its first Student Naturalist Camp. In November, the Tennessee Ornithological Society, public school teachers and students, and volunteers from all over Mississippi staged the Enchanted Forest Fall Festival at the center, attended by hundreds of school children.[11]

The fifth annual Hummingbird Migration Celebration on the second weekend of September 2004 was a landmark three-day event. Although seventy-five people had come to the first celebration in 1999, a record 6500 attended in 2004. It had become one of the largest Audubon-sponsored nature festivals in the country. The event was launched on Thursday with the release of the first banded hummingbird by Mississippi First Lady Marsha Barbour, followed by a twilight VIP supper on the grounds between the Davis House and the Education Center, with entertainment by the Grammy-award-winning gospel group the Dixie Hummingbirds. The following two days were given over to nature walks and to talks by leading authorities on a range of topics, including dragonflies, amphibians, bats, alligators, and hawks.[12]

Research for this history of the Audubon tract was underway, a brochure about the center had been published, a new foot bridge built by staff and volunteers with materials furnished by Home Depot was completed, and four ecological research projects by nearby universities were ongoing. In spring of 2005, a piece on the center by Alan Huffman was the feature article, spread over five pages, in *Preserva-*

tion, the publication of the National Trust for Historic Preservation. "Strawberry Plains was an opportunity for Audubon to do something unique," Audubon consultant Dr. Phillip Ensley told Huffman, "to couple conservation with the history of a community, to demonstrate man's relation with the land." Based on that vision, Ensley had lobbied for "one of the most ambitious projects that the conservation organization had ever undertaken, a hybrid venture dedicated to restoring Strawberry Plains' environment, preserving its history, and educating the public about both." No attempt would be made to achieve a standard practice of historic preservation, the freezing in the "image of a single historical period." The center would instead interpret all eras of its history.[13]

By the time the *Preservation* article was published, a major historic preservation project was in progress—the relocation of Maj. Josiah Patrick Milledge Stephenson's plantation office to Strawberry Plains Audubon Center. This last remaining antebellum plantation office in the northern region of the state, the building later used from Mack post office, was in a dilapidated state and in danger of being torn down. A McAlexander descendant and Chelius H. Carter, local restoration expert, conceived the plan to save the building. Kevin McAlexander and his family donated the old office to the center, and more than twenty thousand dollars was raised from thirty donors among the local community (including the three local banks), former Holly Springs residents, Shackelford Trust Advisors, Finley cousins, and Stephenson-McAlexander descendants to move the structure from the adjoining plantation carved from the Chickasaw Cession to Strawberry Plains and place it on a replicated foundation. Under the supervision of Carter, who volunteered his time, the 150-year-old neighborhood icon was in place north of the Davis House a few weeks before the fall 2005 Hummingbird Celebration. Plans were made to use it for educational purposes.[14]

The sixth annual hummingbird festival was part of the celebration of the one-hundredth anniversary of the founding of the Audubon Society. The primary speaker was John Flicker, president of the National Audubon Society. Other staff from the national offices, along with various national experts in wildlife also participated. There were significant changes from the year before. An improved system of

Bridge at Strawberry Plains Audubon Center in the fall. Courtesy of
National Audubon Society, Strawberry Plains Audubon Center

parking lots and shuttles carried visitors more efficiently from the
boundaries of the center to the main campus. The VIP dinner on
opening night, "Audubon Under the Stars," was held in its familiar
location on the grounds, where this time scores of large round tables
had been placed, and for the first time the grounds were lighted. It
was an exceptional evening.[15]

The reports issued by the center for the following years reflect
the success and expansion of established programs, as well as further development—the building of a teaching woodland amphitheater (sponsored by Home Depot) and a substantial amphitheater trail
bridge (sponsored by Anderson-Tully), the opening to the public of
an interpretive wetlands area, the establishment of a Native Plants
Cooperative with two annual native plant sales, the expansion of
more special events like Migratory Bird Day in the spring, the beginning of a partnership in new adult programs with Rhodes College

and the University of Mississippi, and the initiation of the Coldwater River Watershed conservation program. A master plan for the center grounds has been completed to make it a major American demonstration site of healthy ecosystems for birds and wildlife. To that end, the immediate priority is the building of a new entrance to the preserve to give Strawberry Plains Audubon Center greater visibility and to facilitate and enhance the visitor's experience.[16]

Thousands have already enjoyed and learned from the multifaceted experiences of this center. The vision of Ruth Finley and Margaret Finley Shackelford for a place to memorialize history and culture and to teach respect and reverence for the natural world has been followed faithfully. Perhaps director Madge Lindsay has put best the conceptualization of this unique place: "The center is not just about history and it's not just about nature. It's about what happens on the land and how to keep it viable for both wildlife and people. It's a departure for Audubon, but it makes sense because the landscape connects us all. The common ground is the ground itself."[17]

APPENDIX A
GENEALOGICAL CHARTS

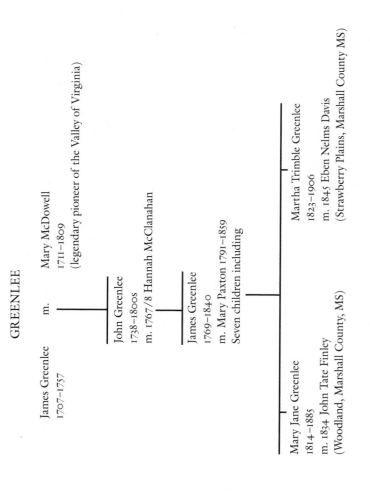

GREENLEE

James Greenlee
1707–1757

m.

Mary McDowell
1711–1809
(legendary pioneer of the Valley of Virginia)

John Greenlee
1738–1800s
m. 1767/8 Hannah McClanahan

James Greenlee
1769–1840
m. Mary Paxton 1791–1859
Seven children including

Mary Jane Greenlee
1814–1885
m. 1834 John Tate Finley
(Woodland, Marshall County, MS)

Martha Trimble Greenlee
1823–1906
m. 1845 Eben Nelms Davis
(Strawberry Plains, Marshall County MS)

FINLEY

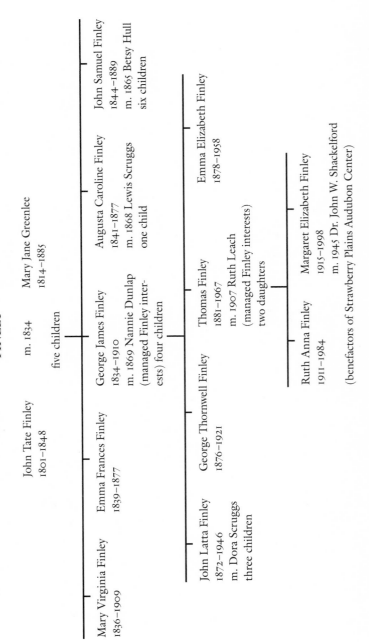

John Tate Finley   m. 1834   Mary Jane Greenlee
1801–1848   five children   1814–1885

Mary Virginia Finley   Emma Frances Finley   George James Finley   Augusta Caroline Finley   John Samuel Finley
1836–1909   1839–1877   1834–1910   1841–1877   1844–1889
                                            m. 1869 Nannie Dunlap m. 1868 Lewis Scruggs   m. 1865 Betsy Hull
                                            (managed Finley inter- one child   six children
                                            ests) four children

John Latta Finley   George Thornwell Finley   Thomas Finley   Emma Elizabeth Finley
1872–1946   1876–1921   1881–1967   1878–1958
m. Dora Scruggs   m. 1907 Ruth Leach
three children   (managed Finley interests)
                                                 two daughters

                                    Ruth Anna Finley   Margaret Elizabeth Finley
                                    1911–1984   1915–1998
                                                            m. 1945 Dr. John W. Shackelford
                                                            (benefactors of Strawberry Plains Audubon Center)

DAVIS

Eben Nelms Davis   m. 1845   Martha Trimble Greenlee
1802–1881   1823–1906
(master of Strawberry Plains)   (heroine of Strawberry Plains)

five children

Eben Nelms Davis Jr.
1847–1935

John Presley Davis
1851–1927
(ran the plantation
for 50 years until
1920s)

Mary Elizabeth Davis
1853–1919
m. 1889 Charles Moseley
one child

Martha V. Moseley
1894–1986
(last of the Davises to live at Strawberry Plains)

Ann Winifred Davis
1856–1935
m. 1874 Presley Stanback
eleven children

Augusta Virginia Davis
1859–1935
m. 1878 Dempsey Brittenum
one son
m. 1886 Robert Johnson
m. 1897 Clarence Greenlee

STEPHENSON

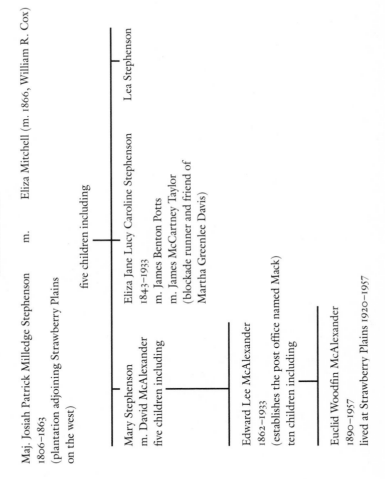

Maj. Josiah Patrick Milledge Stephenson   m.   Eliza Mitchell (m. 1866, William R. Cox)
1806–1863
(plantation adjoining Strawberry Plains
on the west)

five children including

Mary Stephenson   Eliza Jane Lucy Caroline Stephenson   Lea Stephenson
m. David McAlexander   1843–1933
five children including   m. James Benton Potts
                          m. James McCartney Taylor
                          (blockade runner and friend of
                          Martha Greenlee Davis)

Edward Lee McAlexander
1862–1933
(establishes the post office named Mack)
ten children including

Euclid Woodfin McAlexander
1890–1957
lived at Strawberry Plains 1920–1957

MCKISSACK

William McKissack   m.   Janet Susan Cogle Buxton Peters

1781–1855

(financial baron of Maury County, TN,
in 1954 purchased the plantation adjoining
Strawberry Plains on the east)

nine children including

Alexander Cogle McKissack	Jessie Helen McKissack
1831–1898	1838–1921
m. Eliza Aykroyd (1840–1900)	m. 1858 Dr. George B. Peters (who shot and
(leaves McKissack plantation to her sister's son,	killed Confederate general Earl Van Dorn
who dies intestate in 1909, and plantation devolves	because of a reputed liaison between Van Dorn
to his closest kin, his father's siblings and their children)	and his wife)

PROMINENT AFRICAN AMERICAN LINES FROM STEPHENSON SLAVE FAMILIES

Among the slaves held by Maj. Josiah Patrick Milledge Stephenson were the following three, who were probably siblings.

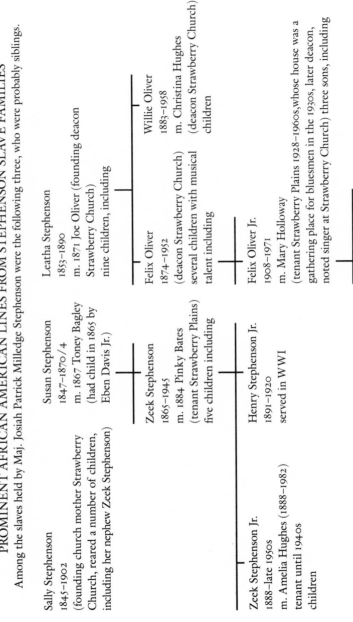

Sally Stephenson
1845–1902
(founding church mother Strawberry Church, reared a number of children, including her nephew Zeek Stephenson)

Susan Stephenson
1847–1870/4
m. 1867 Toney Bagley
(had child in 1865 by Eben Davis Jr.)

Zeek Stephenson
1865–1945
m. 1884 Pinky Bates
(tenant Strawberry Plains) five children including

Zeek Stephenson Jr.
1888–late 1950s
m. Amelia Hughes (1888–1982)
tenant until 1940s children

Henry Stephenson Jr.
1891–1920
served in WWI

Leatha Stephenson
1853–1890
m. 1871 Joe Oliver (founding deacon Strawberry Church)
nine children, including

Felix Oliver
1874–1952
(deacon Strawberry Church) several children with musical talent including

Felix Oliver Jr.
1908–1971
m. Mary Holloway
(tenant Strawberry Plains 1928–1960s, whose house was a gathering place for bluesmen in the 1930s, later deacon, noted singer at Strawberry Church) three sons, including

Felce (Fierce) Oliver
1927–2000
(noted singer and usher at Strawberry Church, valued employee of Martha Moseley in her later years)

Willie Oliver
1883–1958
m. Christina Hughes
(deacon Strawberry Church) children

APPENDIX B
THE CEMETERIES

The Davis Family Cemetery

This cemetery is located 300 meters northwest of the Davis House on a high bluff cut by the branch of the Coldwater River running near the western boundary of the property.

Marked graves

Elizabeth Davis, wife of W. J. Davis, December 19, 1774–August 19, 1842
Willie J. Davis, December 25, 1777–April 22, 1845
Willie Greenlee Davis, son of E. N. and M. T. Davis, January 11, 1846–July 13, 1847
Henry Ann Eliza Phillips, wife of J. L. Phillips, February 1, 1825–November 30, 1847 [she was the daughter of Winifred Davis (sister of Willie J. Davis) and Henry Yarbrough]
Robert Charles Davis, son of E. N. and M. T. Davis, September 14, 1849–August 6, 1850
Emma Frances Davis, daughter of E. N. and M. T. Davis, May 9, 1857–July 24, 1858
Eben Nelms Davis, June 22, 1802–January 14, 1881

Known unmarked graves

An unknown Civil War soldier who died while the schoolroom was being used as a hospital after the battle of Shiloh
Martha Trimble Greenlee Davis, April 20, 1823–January 16, 1906
Charles Pulaski Moseley, November 25, 1860–July 14, 1909
Mary Elizabeth Davis Moseley, July 28, 1853–1919
John Presley Davis, October 23, 1851–November 24, 1927
Eben Nelms Davis Jr., July 28, 1847–July 17, 1935

The Strawberry Plains Slave and Sharecropper Cemetery

This cemetery is located on the ridge southwest of the Davis House. It is accessible from the main road via a path up the ridge that begins immediately southeast of the bridge.

Marked graves

Rachel, wife of Mack Fennell, died December 13, 1885, aged 72 years
Malissie E., wife of B. M. Johnson, September 17, 1867–June 3, 1890

Known unmarked graves

It has been speculated that there are at least sixteen unidentified graves, and among them are probably the following.

Frank Lee, born January 1840, died between 1900 and 1910
Margaret Lee, born January 1835, died between 1900 and 1910
Some members of the Hunt family, who were Davis slaves, including Skeet Hunt, who died before 1935 and is said to have had a tombstone
Hilton Marr, stepson of Ernest Perkins, died circa 1933

The Gibbons Family Cemetery

This cemetery, once a part of the Finley holding, is now on land owned by the North Mississippi Agricultural Experiment Station on Section 17, Range 2, Township 3. It is on the west side of the Highway 7 right of way, to the south of the experiment station buildings.

Marked graves

Amanda A. Stratton, September 14, 1816–June 9, 1847 [daughter of John C. and Jane Graves Gibbons]
John D. Gibbons, December 28, 1836–June 12, 1860 [son of John C. and Jane Graves Gibbons]
Mary A. Moseley, July 3, 1817–August 14, 1886, wife of G. H. Moseley [she was the paternal grandmother of Martha V. Moseley, who was living near the Gibbons place at the time of her death]

Known unmarked graves

John C. Gibbons, born in Delaware 1792, died 1853

The Abandoned Finley Grove Cemetery

This cemetery is located near the southeast corner of Section 8, Range 2, Township 3.

Marked graves

Peter Brannon, died March 15, 1930
Connie Mae Garrison, November 10, 1923–June 20, 1936

NOTES

Abbreviations

AM/SPF: Audubon Mississippi/Strawberry Plains Finley Collection, Special Collections, John Davis Williams Library, University of Mississippi
SPAC: Strawberry Plains Audubon Center
SPOHP: Strawberry Plains/Audubon Mississippi Oral History Project (funded by SPAC and the Mississippi Humanities Council), conducted by the Center for the Study of Southern Culture at the University of Mississippi, transcribed by and housed in the Center for Oral History and Cultural Heritage, University of Southern Mississippi

Chapter 1. The Deep Past

1. Charles Hudson, *Knights of Spain, Warriors of the Sun: Hernando de Soto and the South's Ancient Chiefdoms* (Athens: University of Georgia Press, 1997), 65–67, 257–274.

2. James H. Malone, *The Chickasaw Nation* (Louisville, Ky.: John P. Morton & Co., 1922), 95–98, 289–291; Charles Hudson, Marvin T. Smith, and Chester B. DePrater, "The Hernando de Soto Expedition from Mabila to the Mississippi River," in *Towns and Temples along the Mississippi River*, ed. David H. Dye and Cheryl Anne Cox (Tuscaloosa: University of Alabama Press, 1990), 200–202; Joyce Rockwood Hudson, *Looking for de Soto: A Search through the South for the Spaniard's Trail* (Athens: University of Georgia Press, 1993), 110–125; Hudson, *Knights of Spain*, 66–69.

3. James R. Atkinson, *Splendid Land, Splendid People: The Chickasaw Indians to Removal* (Tuscaloosa: University of Alabama Press, 2004), 11–12; Arrell M. Gibson, *The Chickasaws* (Norman: University of Oklahoma Press, 1971), 25–29; Du Pratz quoted in Samuel Cole Williams's 1930 edition of *Adair's History of the American Indian* (reprint New York: Promontory Press, 1974), 341–342.

4. Atkinson, *Splendid Land*, 143, 17, 91, 279, 188.

5. Jesse D. Jennings, "Nutt's Trip to the Chickasaw Country," *Journal of Mississippi History* 9 (Jan 1947), 45; Hubert H. McAlexander, "The Saga of a Mixed-Blood Chickasaw Dynasty," *Journal of Mississippi History* 49 (Nov 1987), 289–290; Cornelia Pelham letter, quoted in Robert Milton Winter (ed.), *Shadow of a Might Rock: A Social and Cultural History of Presbyterianism in Marshall County, Mississippi* (Franklin, Tenn.: Providence House, 1997), 30; map of Township 4, Range 3 West, 8 Sept 1834, Marshall County Chancery Clerk's Office, Holly Springs; see also Marie King Garland, *Chickasaw Loves and Allied Families* (Ardmore, Okla.: Ardmore Photocopy Co., 1970).

6. 1834 map of Township 3, Range 2, West of the Base Meridian, Chancery Clerk's Office, Holly Springs; Dr. Shipp is quoted in Cyrus Shipp, "Dr. Felix Grundy Shipp," *Yalobusha County History by the Heritage Committee of the Yalobusha Historical Society* (Dallas, Tex.: National ShareGraphics, Inc., 1982), F283.

7. "Some War Incidents and Other Things That Occurred on this Side of the River," unsigned and undated memoir, typescript in Marshall County Historical Museum, 2–3.

8. McAlexander, "The Saga of a Mixed-Blood Chickasaw Dynasty," 290–291.

9. Marshall County Board of Police minutes, 20 April 1836, Chancery Clerk's Office.

10. Robert Milton Winter (ed.), *Amid Some Excellent Company* (Holly Springs, Miss.: Spring Hollow Publishers, 2003), 181; John E. Parsons (ed.), "Letters on the Chickasaw Removal of 1837," *New York Historical Society Quarterly* 37 (Jul 1953), 278–279; Martha V. Moseley, interview by author, 17 Dec 1981.

11. McAlexander, "Flush Times in Holly Springs," *Journal of Mississippi History* 48 (Feb 1986), 2–5.

12. Sectional indexes for Section 12, Township 3, Range 3, and for Sections 7, 8, 17, 18, in Township 3, Range 2, Chancery Clerk's Office; Jackson *Mississippian*, 27 May 1836; Board of Police minutes, 6 Jul 1836. For information on these speculators, see Mary Elizabeth Young, *Redskins, Ruffleshirts, and Rednecks* (Norman: University of Oklahoma Press, 1961).

13. McAlexander, "Flush Times," 6–8; Woodville (Miss.) *Republican*, 6 May 1837.

Chapter 2. The Finleys

1. United Daughters of the Confederacy membership papers of Mary Virginia Finley Goodwyn, 20 Sept 1935, AM/SPF; Joseph A. Waddell, *Annals of Augusta County, Virginia* (1902; 2nd ed., Harrisonburg, Va.: C. J. Carrier Co., 1972), 40, 52, 311–312; J. Lewis Peyton, *History of Augusta County, Virginia*, 2nd ed. (Harrisonburg, Va.: C. J. Carnier Co., 1972), 312–313; *Washington and Lee University Alumni Directory, 1749–1949* (Lexington, Va.: Washington and Lee Alumni, Inc., 1949).

2. "The Seven Hills of Rockbridge," *Rockbridge County, Virginia Heritage Book, 1778–1997* (Walworth, Wis.: B&B Publishing, 1997), 120–121; David M. Dudka, "The Seven Hills: The Mansions of Rockbridge County," senior thesis, Washington and Lee University, Lexington, Va., 1981; H. Middleton Raynal, "The Meeting House by the Falling Spring," *Proceedings of the Rockbridge Historical Society* 10 (1983), 221–235.

3. "Greenlee Landing: A Short History," unsigned and undated typescript, and an extract of 17 Aug 1817 letter from Cornelia Randolph to Virginia Randolph, both in possession of the van Ravenswaay family of Greenlee's Ferry, courtesy of Lisa van Ravenswaay.

4. Oren F. Morton, *A History of Rockbridge County, Virginia* (Staunton, Va., 1920; reprint, Baltimore, Md.: Regional Publishing Co., 1980), 254–256;

James W. McClung, *Historical Significance of Rockbridge County, Virginia* (Staunton, Va.: McClure Co., 1939), 228; Ralph Stebbins Greenlee and Robert Lemuel Greenlee, *Genealogy of the Greenlee Families* (Chicago, 1908), 222–229.

5. Greenlee and Greenlee, *Genealogy of the Greenlee Families*, 243. George Finley's tombstone in Hill Crest Cemetery, Holly Springs, is inscribed with the erroneous birth year 1838.

6. Dr. James Somerville, quoted in David Hackett Fischer and James C. Kelly, *Bound Away: Virginia and the Western Movement* (Charlottesville: University Press of Virginia, 2000), 140; Greenlee and Greenlee, *Genealogy of the Greenlee Families*, 243.

7. This and all other letters from John Tate Finley to his brother-in-law James Dorman Davidson of Lexington, Virginia, are in the Davidson Papers, McCormick Collection, Wisconsin State Historical Society, Madison.

8. Minutes of the Holly Springs Presbyterian Church, 5, photocopy in McAlexander Collection; Finley to Davidson, 2 Jul 1837 and 17 Sept 1837.

9. Finley to Davidson, 17 Sept 1837.

10. John T. Finley to Sam [Finley], 9 Sept 1838, and Finley to Davidson, 17 Nov 1838, both Davidson Papers.

11. Finley to Davidson, 17 Nov 1838; McAlexander, "Flush Times," 1–15; Finley to Davidson, 10 Jun 1839; Holly Springs *Guard*, 12 Jan 1842; *Holly Springs Gazette*, 4 Nov 1842; Deed Book H, 402–403.

12. Finley to Davidson, 10 Jun 1839.

13. *Marshall County Republican*, 28 Sept 1839; Finley to Davidson, 23 Jan 1840.

14. Greenlee and Greenlee, *Genealogy of the Greenlee Families*, 232; Finley to Davidson, 6 Nov 1843 and 23 Jan 1840; William Baskerville Hamilton, *Holly Springs, Mississippi, to the Year 1878* (Holly Springs, Miss.: Marshall County Historical Society, 1984), 9.

Chapter 3. The Davises

1. Finley to James D. Davidson, 6 Nov 1843 and 31 Mar 1845, Davidson Papers, McCormick Collection.

2. Seth Yarbrough Young III, "Davis Family Tree" (unpublished essay), courtesy of author; Hubert H. McAlexander and Ellnora Lancaster Rose Young, *Southside Virginia Skein* (Baltimore, Md.: Gateway Press, 2005), 220.

3. Davis genealogical file, in Young collection.

4. Deed Book M, 261, Marshall County Chancery Clerk's office; Herbert Anthony Kellar (ed.), *Solon Robinson, Pioneer and Agriculturist: Selected Writings* (New York: Da Capo Press, 1968), vol. 1, 448–449; 1850 Marshall County Agricultural Census, 153.

5. Nineteenth-century Southerners loved titles, and men were often addressed by the highest militia title they had ever held. Wealthy planters were also frequently given the honorific title of colonel. In genealogical studies of the Clopton and Clayton families, there is no evidence that either of these men held a military title, and William McAlexander might at some time have served

as justice of the peace, but he had no legal training. Clayton genealogical file accumulated by Margaret M. Nash; Lucy Lane Erwin, *William Clopton of York County, Virginia* (Rutland, Vt.: Tuttle Publishing Co., 1939); Hubert H. McAlexander, *McAlexander: A Family History* (Rockland, Maine: Penobscot Press, 2002), 175–177.

6. Edwin Sawyer Walker (ed.), *Genealogical Notes of the Carpenter Family, Including the Autobiography and Personal Reminiscences of Dr. Seymour D. Carpenter* (Springfield: Illinois State Journal Co., 1907), 95–96.

7. Martha Davis's granddaughter Martha Virginia Moseley (1894–1986) could tell me only that the original house was log. Walker (ed.), *Genealogical Notes of the Carpenter Family*, 96.

8. McAlexander and Young, *Southside Virginia Skein*, 38–40.

9. Reid Smith, *Majestic Middle Tennessee* (Gretna, La.; Pelican, 1982), 76–78; William K. Hall, *Descendants of Nicholas Perkins of Virginia* (Ann Arbor, Mich., 1957).

10. Finley to Davidson, 31 Mar 1845; Hamilton, *Holly Springs, Mississippi*, 76.

11. "The Register of Wesley Chapel Methodist Church (1837–1947)" in Mavis P. Kelsey, *Samuel Kelso/Kelsey* (Houston, Tex., 1984), 587–600; Martha V. Moseley, interview by author, 28 Dec 1980; Walker (ed.), *Genealogical Notes of the Carpenter Family*, 97–99.

Chapter 4. Woodland and Strawberry Plains

1. Eben N. Davis to James D. Davidson, 30 April 1848, Davidson Papers, McCormick Collection.

2. John T. Finley estate papers, Chancery Packet no. 662, Marshall County Chancery Clerk's Office.

3. Receipt for burning of seventy-five thousand bricks for E. N. Davis by Benjamin Davenport, 26 Jun 1848, AM/SPF.

4. William Bartram, *The Travels of William Bartram*, ed. Francis Harper (Athens: University of Georgia Press, 1998), 636; James Adair, *The History of the American Indians*, ed. Kathryn E. Holland Braund (Tuscaloosa: University of Alabama Press, 2005), 439; Malone, *The Chickasaw Nation*, 200. The only letter to James D. Davidson that Eben Davis headed "Strawberry Plains" is dated 15 Aug 1859. When the property was offered to the National Audubon Society in 1982, the wish was expressed that "the name 'Strawberry Plains' be incorporated in the name of the proposed facility or preserve" (statement attached to letter of Robert P. Crutcher to W. Carlyle Blakeney Jr., National Audubon Society, both dated 20 Oct 1982, SPAC).

5. 1850 Marshal County census slave schedule and agricultural schedule, Eben N. Davis entries; E. N. Davis lumber account with C. L. Martin, Aug–Dec 1851, paid in full 24 Dec 1851, AM/SPF.

6. E. N. Davis account with A. T. Wells, Memphis, 25 Nov 1852, AM/SPF.

7. Red cedars were commonly used in Marshall County plantation landscaping at the big house. An especially large grove of the trees near the road fronting

the nearby Williams-Dawson plantation house stood for almost a hundred years. That place, unoccupied after 1870 and subsequently in ruins, may well have been named Cedar Grove, the name often used (in lowercase) as a reference point in the neighborhood. The neighboring Stephenson place had a single avenue of cedars lining a wide brick walk from the road to the front portico. The most impressive example of such landscaping in the county was at Woodlawn near the crossroads of Marianna southwest of Holly Springs. Three towering, very long avenues filled the yard in front of a sprawling one-story plantation house. In the town of Holly Springs, one such planting still survives at Wakefield on Salem Avenue.

8. The portrait of the plantation and its mistress is drawn from Hubert H. McAlexander, "Strawberry Plains: House of History," *South Reporter*, 19 Jun 1958; William H. Duncan, "A Brief Account of the Life of Martha Trimble Greenlee Davis (1823–1906)," written in fall 1979 for a graduate folklore course at the University of Arkansas, Little Rock; and map of Strawberry Plains plantation, drawn in 1965 by Hubert H. McAlexander as directed by Martha Virginia Moseley, all in AM/S PF.

9. A. M. Clayton, *Centennial Address on the History of Marshall County* (Washington, D.C., 1880); Robert Milton Winter (ed.), *Our Pen Is Time: The Diary of Emma Finley* (Lafayette, Calif.: Thomas-Berryhill Press, 1999).

10. Eben N. Davis to James D. Davidson, 9 April and 13 May 1856, Davidson Papers, McCormick Collection.

Chapter 5. The Slaves

1. Slaves schedules of the 1860 U.S. Census for Marshall County, Mississippi, 46.

2. John Hebron Moore, *The Emergence of the Cotton Kingdom in the Old Southwest: Mississippi, 1770–1860* (Baton Rouge: Louisiana State University Press, 1988), 108; Eugene D. Genovese, *Roll, Jordan, Roll: The World the Slaves Made* (New York: Random House, 1974), 328; Duncan, "A Brief Account," AM/SPF; Winter (ed.), *Our Pen Is Time*, 70. I have also drawn upon my own "Strawberry Plains: House of History," in the 19 Jun 1958, Holly Springs *South Reporter*, and corrected some mistakes made there almost fifty years ago.

3. Moore, *Emergence of the Cotton Kingdom*, 108; McAlexander, "Strawberry Plains"; narrative of Aaron Jones, in George P. Rawick (ed.), *The American Slave: A Composite Autobiography*, Supplement Ser. I, vol. 8, *Mississippi Narratives* (Westport, Conn.: Greenwood Press, 1977), 1185–1186; William Kaufman Scarborough, *Masters of the Big House: Elite Slaveholders of the Mid-Nineteenth-Century South* (Baton Rouge: Louisiana State University Press, 2003), 201; Clara Clayton Fant, "Away Down in Dixie," 1885 manuscript, photocopy in McAlexander Collection, 2; Seymour Carpenter, quoted in Walker (ed.), *Genealogical Notes of the Carpenter Family*, 96.

4. Henry Morton Woodson, *The Woodsons and Their Connections* (Memphis, 1915), 301, 465; Booker Flippin contract, AM/SPF; Genovese, *Roll, Jordan,*

Roll, 365–366. Eben Davis's granddaughter Martha V. Moseley had apparently confused "overseer" and "driver" when she told me in the 1950s that Strawberry Plains had a slave overseer.

5. Rawick (ed.), *The American Slave*, vol. 8, 864.

6. E. N. Davis to James D. Davidson, 9 April 1856, and 14 Aug 1858, Davidson Papers, McCormick Collection; James M. Power, typescript of memoir of his mother, McAlexander Collection, 93, 102; Ben Robertson, *Red Hills and Cotton* (New York: Alfred A. Knopf, 1942), 222–223; sectional index for Section 26, Township 2, Range 3, Deed Book O, 44, Chancery Clerk's Office; Walker (ed.), *Genealogical Notes of the Carpenter Family*, 98.

7. 1860 Marshall County slave schedules, 95B; Fant, "Away Down South in Dixie," 4; McAlexander, "Strawberry Plains."

8. Moore, *Emergence of the Cotton Kingdom*, 104.

9. Fant, "Away Down South in Dixie," 5; McAlexander, "Strawberry Plains"; Duncan, "A Brief Account," AM/SPF.

10. Winter (ed.), *Our Pen Is Time*, 32; Genovese, *Roll, Jordan, Roll*, 475–481; Fant, "Away Down South in Dixie," 4–5.

11. Sylvia Floyd, quoted in Moore, *Emergence of the Cotton Kingdom*, 104; Fant, "Away Down South in Dixie," 6–7.

12. Fant, "Away Down South in Dixie," 7.

13. Rawick (ed.), *The American Slave*, vol. 8, 1187, vol. 6, 264–265, vol. 7, 350–351, 366; Moore, *Emergence of the Cotton Kingdom*, 110; Walker (ed.), *Genealogical Notes of the Carpenter Family*, 100; Rawick (ed.), *The American Slave*, vol. 8, 1186, vol. 7, 365–366, vol. 8, 1052.

14. Davis to Davidson, 17 Feb 1855, Davidson Papers, McCormick Collection.

15. Davis to Davidson, 9 April 1856, McCormick Collection.

16. Davis to Davidson, 14 Aug 1858, McCormick Collection.

Chapter 6. War

1. Marshall County Deed Book X, 281, Book 27, 427; Herbert Weaver, *Mississippi Farmers, 1850–1860* (Nashville: Vanderbilt University Press, 1945), 112.

2. E. N. Davis to Greenlee Davidson, 21 Nov 1859, Davidson Papers, McCormick Collection; St. Thomas Hall catalogue for 1895–1896 (in the possession of Chesley Thorne Smith, Holly Springs); *Journal of the Protestant Episcopal Convention of the Diocese of Mississippi 1861* (Jackson: Mississippian Book and Job Office, 1861), 23; "Seven Civil War Battles Recalled in Yazoo Soldier's Memoirs," *Yazoo Daily Herald* (Yazoo City, Miss., undated clipping), B8.

3. Robert Milton Winter (ed.), *Amid Some Excellent Company: Holly Springs, Mississippi, Through the Life and Words of John M. Mickle* (Holly Springs, Miss.: Spring Hollow Publishers, 2003), 81–82; James W. Silver (ed.), *A Life for the Confederacy as Recorded in the Pocket Diaries of Pvt. Robert A. Moore* (Jackson, Tenn.: McCowat-Mercer Press, 1959), 21; Karlem Riess, "Claudius Wistar Sears, Soldier and Educator," *Journal of Mississippi History* 11 (April 1949), 128–137.

4. John S. Finley to Martha Greenlee Davis, 24 Jul 1861, AM/SPF; Woodson, *The Woodsons and Their Connections*, 465.

5. John M. Mickle, "Holly Springs in the War between the States," Mississippi *Baptist Record*, 3 Dec 1936, 3; deposition of Eliza Stephenson Potts Taylor for Davis Civil War claim, 21 Jan 1901, McAlexander Collection; advertisement for cotton tie and Theo Duval to Col. E. N. Davis, 28 Jan 1862, both in AM/SPF.

6. Hubert H. McAlexander, *The Prodigal Daughter: A Biography of Sherwood Bonner* (Baton Rouge: Louisiana State University Press, 1981), 12; Mildred Thomson Strickland to Capt. William M. Strickland, 9 Mar 1862, typescript of Strickland letters, McAlexander Collection; Martha Neville Lumpkin (ed.), *"Dear Darling Loulie": Letters of Cordelia Lewis Scales to Loulie W. Irby during and after the War between the States*, 2nd ed. (Clarksville, Tenn., 1980), 34–38; McAlexander, "Strawberry Plains."

7. Marshall County Deed Book D, 12, Book L, 418; 1840 Marshall County census, 37; Betty C. Wiltshire (ed.), *Marshall County, Mississippi, Probate and Will Records* (Carrollton. Miss.: Pioneer Publishing Co., 1996), 161–166; Josephine McGowan Cox, "Gibbons-Roberts-McGowan History," unnumbered typescript in Virginia Woodson Carter Historical Room, Holly Springs Presbyterian Church; Winter (ed.), *Our Pen Is Time*, 59.

8. McAlexander, "Flush Times," 8.

9. William T. Sherman, *Memoirs of Gen. W. T. Sherman* (New York: Charles L. Webster & Co., 1892), vol. 1, 285–286; Brooks D. Simpson and Jean V. Berlin (eds.), *Sherman's Civil War: Selected Correspondence of William T. Sherman, 1860–1865* (Chapel Hill: University of North Carolina Press, 1999), 245–246; William S. Speer, "Gen. William H. Jackson," *Sketches of Prominent Tennesseans* (Nashville: Albert B. Tavel, 1888), 447; Sherman, *Memoirs*, 286.

10. Sherman to Maj. John A. Rawlins, 8 Jul 1862, *Official Records of the War of the Rebellion*, ser. 1, vol. 17, pt. 2, 85; Josephine McGowan Cox, "Gibbons-Roberts-McGowan History," unnumbered.

11. Memphis *Daily Appeal*, 1 Jul 1862, 2; Sherman, *Memoirs*, 286; Simpson and Berlin (eds.), *Selected Correspondence of William T. Sherman*, 249.

12. James M. McPherson, *Battle Cry of Freedom* (New York: Oxford University Press, 1988), 418; Sherman, *Memoirs*, 294; Simpson and Berlin (eds.), *Selected Correspondence of William T. Sherman*, 260–261; Mildred Strickland to Capt. William M. Strickland, 8 Jun [1862], McAlexander Collection; Duncan, "A Brief Account," 9, AM/SPF. For stories of women running the blockade, see Robert Burrell Alexander diary, 1861–1865, photocopy in possession of Dr. Robert Emmon Tyson of Holly Springs, and Sherwood Bonner, "From '60 to '65," *Lippincott's Magazine* 18 (Oct 1876), 505–509.

13. Sherman, *Memoirs*, 288; Arthur B. Carter, *The Tarnished Cavalier: Major General Earl Van Dorn* (Knoxville: University of Tennessee Press, 1999), 85, 107.

14. Maury statement quoted in Carter, *Tarnished Cavalier*, 4; Marshall County Deed Book U, 167, Book W, 395; *Maury County Cousins: Bible and Family Records*, comp. Maury County (Nashville: Tennessee Historical Society, 1967), 175.

15. Jill K. Garrett (comp.), *Obituaries from Tennessee Newspapers* (Easley, S.C.: Southern Historical Press, 1980), 294; Mrs. Dr. G. B. Peters [Jessie McKissack Peters] to Mr. Cheairs, Mar [18]60, Figuers Collection, 1985 Addition, Tennessee State Library and Archives, Nashville.

16. David E. Roth, "The Mysteries of Spring Hill, Tennessee," *Blue and Gray* 2 (Oct/Nov 1984), 14; Jill K. Garrett and Marise P. Lightfoot, *The Civil War in Maury County, Tennessee* (Columbia, Tenn., 1966), 225; obituary of Alexander C. McKissack, *The Confederate Veteran* 7 (Jan 1899), 33; Jennifer W. Ford (ed.), "'Our Precious Little Circle': The Enduring Strength of Family and Community in the Civil War Letters of William Cowper Nelson" (typescript to be published by University of Tennessee Press), 90, 103, 319.

17. John Bennett Boddie, "Boddie Family," *Historical Southern Families* (Baltimore, Md.: Genealogical Publishing Co., 1957), vol. 1, 345–350. The story that members of the McKissack family had been refugees in Holly Springs during the war was repeated to me in the 1950s by Clara Carr Olson, whose grandmother was named McKissack and who was told the story forty years before.

18. Lumpkin (ed.), *Dear Darling Loulie*, 43–44; Bonner, "From '60 to '65," 505–509.

19. Sherman to Maj. Rawlins, 21 Oct 1862, *Official Records*, ser. 1, vol. 17, pt. 2, 286–287; Carter, *Tarnished Cavalier*, 114–115; Bonner, "From '60 to '65," 506.

20. Jackson to Van Dorn, 5 Nov 1862, *Official Records*, ser. 1, vol. 17, pt. 2, 902.

Chapter 7. The Two Armies

1. Lumpkin (ed.), *Dear Darling Loulie*, 51–52; Bruce Catton, *Grant Moves South* (Boston: Little, Brown, 1960), 328–330; Carter, *Tarnished Cavalier*, 120–122; *Official Records*, ser. 1, vol. 17, pt. 1, 488.

2. Memphis *Daily Appeal*, 27 Nov 1862, 2, col. 5.

3. George Cadman to Esther Cadman, 23 Nov 1862, George Cadman Papers, Southern Historical Collection, University of North Carolina; Peter Casey to his wife, 7 Jan 1863, Peter Casey File, Chicago Historical Society.

4. James Swan, "Chicago's Irish Legion: The 90th Illinois in the American Civil War," typescript courtesy of Professors James and Patricia Swan, 39.

5. George H. Woodruff, *Fifteen Years Ago: Or the Patriotism of Will County* (Joliet, Ill.: Joliet Republican Printing House, 1876), 372–373; Swan, "Chicago's Irish Legion," 45–48.

6. Carter, *Tarnished Cavalier*, 138–146; narrative of Aaron Jones, in Rawick (ed.), *The American Slave*, vol. 8, 1186.

7. Carter, *Tarnished Cavalier*, 129, 157; Bonner, "From '60 to '65," 503.

8. John Y. Simon (ed.), *The Papers of Ulysses S. Grant* (Carbondale: Southern Illinois Press, 1977), vol. 7, 76–91; Benjamin P. Thomas (ed.), *Three Years with Grant as Recalled by War Correspondent Sylvanus Cadwallader* (New York: Alfred A. Knopf, 1956), 38–40; Ulysses S. Grant, *Personal Memoirs* (New York: Charles L. Webster & Co., 1885), 438; *Official Records*, ser. 1, vol. 17, pt. 1, 480.

9. David Habura (ed.), *The Fletcher Pomeroy Civil War Diary* (Olympia, Wa., n.d.), 22; claim of Josiah M. Stephenson (no. 768 Congressional), copy in McAlexander Collection.

10. Duncan, "A Brief Account," 6–7, AM/SPF.

11. Deposition of Eliza Jane Stephenson Potts Taylor for Davis Civil War claim, 21 Jan 1901, McAlexander Collection; 1860 Marshall County Agricultural

Census, 1, no. 5; Mary Barton Clark to E. N. Davis, 28 Mar 1862, and E. J. McKissack to E. N. Davis, both in AM/SPF.

12. *Official Records*, ser. 1, vol. 17, pt. 1, 487–488; P. A Willis to S. E. Carey, Harvey W. Walter Papers, no. 3399, Southern Historical Collection, University of North Carolina, Chapel Hill; Charles Waldo, letter to the West Bend, Wisconsin, *Post*, 14 Feb 1863, 2, cols. 2–3, posted by Russell Scott at www.rsscott. com; Mildred Strickland to Capt. William M. Strickland, 16 Jan 1863, typescript in McAlexander Collection.

13. Carter, *Tarnished Cavalier*, 161–163, 167.

14. Carter, *Tarnished Cavalier*, 177–178.

15. John R. Peacock to Miss Irene Cheairs of Spring Hill, 21 Jun 1954, John R. Peacock to Mrs. Wharton J. Cheairs, 3 Sept 1963, and Hugh Walker to Mrs. Cheairs, 24 Jul 1963 (this mailing also contains a copy of a letter about the Van Dorn murder from D. B. Starke to Jefferson Davis in the Duke University Library), all in Figuers Collection, 1985 Addition, Tennessee State Library and Archives; Roth, "The Mysteries of Spring Hill, Tennessee," 15; Garrett and Lightfoot, *The Civil War in Maury County, Tennessee*, 224–225.

16. Carter, *Tarnished Cavalier*, 182–183.

17. Dr. Peters's statement to Union Army police in Nashville, quoted from *Annals of the Army of the Cumberland*, 618–620, in Garrett (comp.), *Obituaries from Tennessee Newspapers*, 291–292; Carter, *Tarnished Cavalier*, 186–187.

Chapter 8. Devastation

1. Grant, *Personal Memoirs*, 436; Habura (ed.), *The Fletcher Pomeroy Civil War Diary*, 24; Mildred Strickland to Capt. William M. Strickland, 16 Jan 1863, typescript in McAlexander Collection.

2. P. A. Willis to S. E. Carey, 3 Feb 186[3], Harvey W. Walter Papers, no. 3399, Southern Historical Collection, University of North Carolina, Chapel Hill; *Official Records*, ser. 1, vol. 17, pt. 1, 470–471; Catton, *Grant Moves South*, 358–363; Grant, *Personal Memoirs*, vol. 1, 426.

3. John Eaton, *Grant, Lincoln, and the Freedman* (New York: Longsman, Green, and Co., 1907), 19; George Cadman to Esther Cadman, 5 Jan 1863, George Cadman Papers, Southern Historical Collection, University of North Carolina, Chapel Hill.

4. This dramatic exodus of thousands of slaves has been captured most vividly not in historical documents, but in William Faulkner's work *The Unvanquished* (New York: Random House, 1938). Historian Don Harrison Doyle was the first to connect the cavalcade marching to Grand Junction with Faulkner's fiction in *Faulkner's Country: The Historical Roots of Yoknapatawpha* (Chapel Hill: University of North Carolina Press, 2001), 220–221. Mildred Strickland to Capt. William M. Strickland, 16 Jan 1863, typescript in McAlexander Collection; Robert Burrell Alexander diary, 12 Feb 1863, in possession of Dr. Robert Emmon Tyson of Holly Springs.

5. Alexander diary, 12 Feb 1863; McAlexander, "Strawberry Plains."

6. Eaton, *Grant, Lincoln, and the Freedman*, 47–48, 51; Alexander diary, 15

Feb 1863; Habura (ed.), *Fletcher Pomeroy Civil War Diary*, 1 Feb 1863, 25; typescript of Strickland letters, McAlexander Collection, 25 Jan and 2 Feb 1863.

7. Duncan, "A Brief Account," 7, AM/SPF; 1863–1864 Eben N. Davis tax receipt, AM/SPF. In the 1950s, Netty Fant Thompson and Mary Seale Sanderson, descendants of these planters, told me of their forebears' moving with their slaves to Texas.

8. Jim Power to Bobby Mitchell, 16 Nov 2005, courtesy of Bobby Mitchell; Ben. C. Gray, "Scouting by Some of Morgan's Men," *Confederate Veteran* 10 (1903), 161; obituary of Sam Finley, Holly Springs *Reporter*, 25 Jun 1898, 2; letter to Tom and Edmund enclosed in George J. Finley to Eben N. Davis, 18 Sept 1863, AM/SPF; McAlexander, *The Prodigal Daughter*, 14–15.

9. *Official Records*, ser. 1, vol. 17, pt. 1, 507–508; Arthur Palmer Hudson (ed.), *Folksongs of Mississippi and Their Background* (Chapel Hill: University of North Carolina Press, 1936), 264–265; Winter (ed.), *Amid Some Excellent Company*, 186; Duncan, "A Brief Account," 8–9, AM/SPF.

10. Duncan, "A Brief Account," 8, AM/SPF; interview with Martha V. Moseley by author, 24 Nov 1981.

11. R. G. Matthews to Col. R. A. Alston, 6 Dec 1863, John Hunt Morgan Papers, no. 2842, Southern Historical Collection, University of North Carolina, Chapel Hill; Mickle, "Holly Springs in the War between the States," 2.

12. *Official Records*, ser. 1, vol. 32, pt. 2, 68; Marshall County Deed Book 6, 97, Book X, 281; McAlexander, "Strawberry Plains." The shooting is also documented by a letter of Daniel Megginson to his father, 14 Feb 1864, photocopy in possession of Bobby Mitchell, Holly Springs, Miss.

13. Duncan, "A Brief Account," 11–12, AM/SPF.

14. Mildred Strickland to Capt. William M. Strickland, 4 May 1863, typescript in McAlexander Collection; Duncan, "A Brief Account," 15, AM/SPF.

15. Bonner, "From '60 to '65," 509.

Chapter 9. Hard Times

1. Whitelaw Reid, *After the War: A Southern Tour, May 1, 1865, to May 1, 1866* (Cincinnati: Moore, Wilstach, and Baldwin, 1866), 425; Ruth Watkins, "Reconstruction in Marshall County," *Publications of the Mississippi Historical Society* 12 (1912), 158.

2. Author's 1955 transcription of Stephenson slave register, McAlexander Collection.

3. Genovese, *Roll, Jordan, Roll*, 414–415; interview with Lillian Burton and Ruth Shelton, 21 Feb 2004, SPOHP; interview with Martha V. Moseley by author, 25 Nov 1981.

4. Interview with Mary Ann Wilson Stanback by author, 15 Jun 2005; telephone interview with Lillian Burton by author, 1 Jul 2003.

5. Marshall County Deed Book 27, 336; Holly Springs *Reporter* quoted in the Jackson *Daily Clarion and Standard*, 8 May 1866.

6. Jackson *Daily Clarion and Standard*, 1 May 1866; Barbara Tuchman, *A Distant Mirror: The Calamitous 14th Century* (New York: Knopf, 1978), 66.

7. Miss Moseley remembered jousts on the Stephenson field on what was

then the McAlexander place (next to the baseball diamond) as late as 1910; Jackson *Daily Clarion and Standard*, 1 and 7 Jul 1866.

8. "Brief Account of Big Tournament, Glamorous Social Event of 1866," in Winter (ed.), *Amid Some Excellent Company*, 301–303.

9. "Brief Account," in Winter (ed.), *Amid Some Excellent Company*, 303; *Memphis Daily Argus*, 20 Jul 1866.

10. 15 April 1867 millwork receipt in AM/ SPF.

11. Holly Springs *Reporter* quoted in Jackson *Daily Clarion and Standard*, 8 May 1866; E. N. Davis bankruptcy statement, copy of Mary Jane Finley, AM/ SPF; Marshall County Deed Book 27, 427, 336.

12. Lumpkin (ed.), *Dear Darling Loulie*, 177; interview with Martha V. Moseley by author, 10 Jun 1958.

13. William C. Harris, *The Day of the Carpetbagger: Republican Reconstruction in Mississippi* (Baton Rogue: Louisiana State University Press, 1979), 274–276; agricultural schedules 1870 Marshall County census.

14. 1870 Marshall County census, 376; Robert Milton Winter (ed.), *Civil War Women: The Diaries of Belle Strickland and Cora Harris Watson* (Lafayette, Calif.: Thomas-Berryhill Press, 2001), 286.

15. Greenlee and Greenlee, *Genealogy of the Greenlee Families*, 273–274; Sectional Indexes, Sections 27, 28, and 7, Township 3, Range 2, Marshall County Chancery Clerk's Office; Jim Power, *A Respectable Minority in the South during the Civil War* (Bloomington, Ind.: Author-House, 2005), 54–55; Winter (ed.), *Civil War Women*, 98–99; Anne Crump Hull to My Dear Sister, 15 Jul [1863], typescript in McAlexander Collection; Lumpkin (ed.), *Dear Darling Loulie*, 154–155; Winter (ed.), *Amid Some Excellent Company*, 23–24, 53–56.

16. Marshall County Deed Book 45, 439–441; Rockbridge County, Virginia, Deed Book TT, 19–21; John F. Greenlee Papers in MSS 640, Alderman Library, University of Virginia.

Chapter 10. The Freedmen and Strawberry Plains Baptist Church

1. Richard Aubrey McLemore (ed.), *A History of Mississippi* (Hattiesburg, Miss.: University and College Press of Mississippi, 1973), vol. 1, 545; Doyle, *Faulkner's County*, 274; McLemore, *History of Mississippi*, vol. 1, 557; Vernon Lane Wharton, *The Negro in Mississippi, 1865–1890* (Chapel Hill: University of North Carolina Press, 1947), 165.

2. Wharton, *The Negro in Mississippi*, 165–166; Watkins, "Reconstruction in Marshall County," 185; Duncan, "A Brief Account," 14–15, AM/SPF.

3. James Wilford Garner, *Reconstruction in Mississippi* (1901; reprint, Baton Rouge: Louisiana State University Press, 1968), 338; McLemore, *A History of Mississippi*, vol. 1, 566; Watkins, "Reconstruction in Marshall County," 180; Rawick (ed.), *The American Slave*, vol. 7, 377, 347; Watkins, 180; Rawick (ed.), vol. 8, 120, 1188.

4. William C. Harris, *Presidential Reconstruction in Mississippi* (Baton Rouge: Louisiana State University Press, 1967), 160; Wharton, *The Negro in Mississippi*, 59; Rawick (ed.), *The American Slave*, vol. 8, 1208.

5. Robert B. Alexander diaries, entries for 15 and 23 Jun 1865, in possession

of Dr. Robert Emmon Tyson of Holly Springs; Wharton, *The Negro in Missis-sippi*, 74–75; 7 Oct 1865 Freedmen's Bureau contract, McAlexander Collection; National Archives Microfilm Publication M1907, roll 19, vol. 153 (Sept 1867–Dec 1868), 28, Records of the Bureau of Refugees, Freedmen, and Abandoned Lands, Mississippi, 1865–1872, Record Group 105, National Archives, Washington, D.C.

6. Letters sent from Mississippi Freedmen's Bureau, 1867–1868, Holly Springs, Mississippi, roll 19, Record Group 105, National Archives; Roger L. Ransom and Richard Sutch, *One Kind of Freedom: The Economic Consequences of Emancipation* (Cambridge: Cambridge University Press, 1977), 97.

7. Ransom and Sutch, *One Kind of Freedom*, 87; Gavin Wright, *The Political Economy of the Cotton South* (New York: W. W. Norton, 2001), 162; James L. Roark, *Masters without Slaves: Southern Planters in the Civil War and Reconstruction* (New York: W. W. Norton, 1977), 142.

8. Ransom and Sutch, *One Kind of Freedom*, 25.

9. Hubert H. McAlexander, "Rev. McMahon Prominent in Cumberland Church History," *South Reporter Sesquicentennial Issue*, 24 April 1986, 3–4; Wesley Chapel register in Dr. and Mrs. Mavis P. Kelsey, *Samuel Kelso/Kelsey* (Houston, Tex., 1984), 588–600; Homer Worsham, *A Brief History of the Red Banks Baptist Church, 1848–1973* (Red Banks, Miss., 1973), 7, 15.

10. Genovese, *Roll, Jordan, Roll*, 240–241, 213.

11. Anonymous [Dr. Sylvester W. Oliver Jr. and Lula Bell Fennell Oliver Freeman], "Strawberry Missionary Baptist Church History" (1975).

12. For information on the church's founding leaders, I have drawn on Willie H. Mallory's excellent 2006 typescript "'When I Can Read My Title Clear': A History of Strawberry Plains Missionary Baptist Church," my own experience of having grown up among these white and black families, my transcription in the 1950s of the Stephenson slave register, and the following Marshall County census records: 1870, 555–556; 1880, 401–408; 1900, Beat 1, family nos. 34–181.

13. Fannie Jones Martin 2003 interview in Mallory, "When I Can Read My Title Clear," 89–90; Eliza Jane Stephenson Potts Taylor to E. L. McAlexander, 20 Feb 1902, McAlexander Collection.

14. Marshall County Deed Book 40, 324–328, Book 44, 5–6, 107–108.

Chapter 11. The Next Generation

1. Both notices in AM/SPF.

2. Interview with Nell Fitts Beswick by author, 15 Jun 2005; interview with Martha V. Moseley by author, 28 Dec 1980.

3. Stanback genealogical papers in possession of Mary Ann Stanback Wilson, Byhalia, Miss.; John F. Greenlee to Mary Elizabeth Davis, 16 April 1877, AM/SPF; Marshall County Deed Book 41, 516; interview with Nell Fitts Beswick by author, 15 Jun 2005; George J. Finley to John F. Greenlee, 26 May 1879, in Cocke MSS 640, Alderman Library, University of Virginia.

4. Hubert H. McAlexander, *A Southern Tapestry: Marshall County, Missis-*

sippi, 1835–2000 (Virginia Beach: Donning, 2000), 70–72; Winter (ed.), *Amid Some Excellent Company,* 115–128, 34, 321.

5. Interview with Mary Ann Stanback Wilson by author, 9 Jul 2005; "Fatal Railroad Accident," Holly Springs *South,* 11 Mar 1885, 1; Duncan, "A Brief Account," 5, AM/SPF; John F. Greenlee to Virginia Finley, 6 Dec 1887, AM/SPF.

6. Interview with Martha V. Moseley by author, 28 Dec 1980; Marshall County Deed Book 55, 187–189, 194–195, Book 59, 521, Book 72, 470; Winter (ed.), *Amid Some Excellent Company,* 200, 202; William M. Strickland to Belle Strickland Bates, 26 Nov 1891, typescript in McAlexander Collection; William Lincoln Giles, "Agricultural Revolution, 1890–1970," in *A History of Mississippi,* ed. Richard Aubrey McLemore (Hattiesburg: University and College Press of Mississippi, 1973), vol. 2, 178.

7. 1939 obituary of Judge Clarence Greenlee, AM/SPF; interview with Nell Fitts Beswick by author, 15 Jun 2005; 1900 census of Marshall County, Beat 1, family no. 164. Roger Brittenum (1879–1933) subsequently married Mollie Hopson, granddaughter of John L. Hudson, a prominent planter for whose family the village of Hudsonville was named. The Brittenums settled on Hudson land near the village.

8. Petition of George J. Finley to the Second Chancery District of Mississippi on the Scruggs indebtedness, circa 1881, AM/SPF; John S. Finley to George J. Finley, 9 Oct 1881, Finley Collection, Mississippi Department of Archives and History, Jackson.

9. Obituary of John S. Finley, Holly Springs *Reporter,* 18 April 1889; John S. Finley papers and George J. Finley to John P. Davis, 12 April 1889, AM/SPF; Broox Sledge, "The Post Offices of Marshall County," *Marshall Messenger,* 14 Mar 1984; deed from Washington West and Mary B. West to F. S. Scruggs and John S. Finley, founders of the Alabama and Pennsylvania Improvement Company, 1888, AM/SPF; John S. Finley Chancery file no. 2029, Marshall County Chancery Clerk's Office.

10. Petition for John S. Finley's widow in AM/SPF; Lilian Kirk Hammond, "The Young Women of Tippah: A Sketch of Twenty-Five Years Ago," *Atlantic Monthly* 48 (Dec 1911), 846 (photocopy annotated for me by Betsy Hull Finley's granddaughter Bessie Craft Driver in the summer of 1978); "Bill Arp at Holly Springs," Holly Springs *South,* 11 May 1887; E. H. F[inley] to George J. Finley, 6 Aug 1906, AM/SPF.

11. George J. Finley ledgers and financial papers, AM/SPF; appointment of George J. Finley as delegate to National Farmers Congress, 12 Dec 1893, S. M. Tracey, Director of Mississippi Agricultural Experiment State to George J. Finley, 25 Nov 1892 and 21 April 1893, and E. E. Rand to George J. Finley, 5 Jan 1897, all in Mississippi Department of Archives and History, Jackson; Marshall County Deed Book 75, 458.

12. Garrett (comp.), *Obituaries from Tennessee Newspapers,* 261; obituaries of Alexander C. McKissack in Holly Springs *Reporter,* 6 Oct 1898, Holly Springs *South,* 13 Oct 1898, and Memphis *Commercial Appeal,* 29 Sept 1898; Marshall County Deed Book 66, 46.

13. Carter, *Tarnished Cavalier,* 196–197; Roth, "The Mysteries of Spring

Hill, Tennessee," 19–20; Garrett (comp.), *Obituaries from Tennessee Newspapers*, 292–293.

14. *Republican Banner* quoted in Garrett (comp.), *Obituaries from Tennessee Newspapers*, 292; Roth, "The Mysteries of Spring Hill, Tennessee," 19.

15. Edwin Bearss to Patricia Swan, as reported by Swan in email to author, 4 May 2006.

16. Marshall County Deed Book U, 167, Book W, 395, Book 66, 46; A. C. McKissack probate file no. 2510, Marshall County Chancery Clerk's Office.

Chapter 12. A New Century

1. Sledge, "The Post Offices of Marshall County." It is the original plantation office, later the post office, that was moved to SPAC in 2005.

2. Hubert H. McAlexander, "Recollections over Ninety Years" [of Chester E. McAlexander], *South Reporter*, 29 Jun 1978. Note that in 1920 the two post–Civil War Holly Springs newspapers merged.

3. Mallory, "When I Can Read My Title Clear," 22–24.

4. Mallory, "When I Can Read My Title Clear," 30–32; anonymous [Dr. Sylvester W. Oliver Jr. and Lula Bell Oliver Freeman], "Strawberry Missionary Baptist Church," 1975 history.

5. Marshall County Deed Book 46, 338, Book 58, 75–77, 434–435; McAlexander, *A Southern Tapestry*, 108; interview with Whitley Cocke by author, 10 Jan 2006; interview with Brankley Speight by author, 9 Sept 2005; Lillian Wilson Stratmon, "Teer, Landowner and Philanthropist," *South Reporter*, 1 Jun 2000; Louis R. Harlan and Raymond W. Smock (ed.), *The Booker T. Washington Papers* (Urbana: University of Illinois Press, 1981), 67.

6. Duncan, "A Brief Account," AM/SPF; Mrs. E. J. Taylor to E. L. McAlexander, 29 Oct 1920, McAlexander Collection.

7. E. N. Davis Jr. note to George J. Finley, 1 Nov 1897, AM/SPF; John P. Davis and Roger Brittenum signed note to George J. Finley, 3 Jun 1901, AM/SPF; Marshall County Deed Book 73, 319, Book 72, 488, Book 73, 65.

8. Interviews by author with Martha V. Moseley, 28 Dec 1980, and with Nell Fitts Beswick, 15 Jun 2005.

9. Moseley interview, 28 Dec 1980; interview with Nancy Fant Smith by author, 30 Jun 2006; Rev. James Arthur MacClellan Hanna, *The House of Dunlap* (Ann Arbor: Edwards Bros., 1956), 219–220.

10. Marshall County Deed Book 69, 610; George J. Finley obituaries in Holly Springs *South*, 5 Oct 1910, and Holly Springs *Reporter*, 6 Oct 1910; W. A. Jones to George J. Finley, 19 April 1906, AM/SPF.

11. M. McPherson to George J. Finley, 25 Mar 1910, and George T. Finley to A. W. White, 20 Jul 1911, both in the Finley Collection, Mississippi Department of Archives and History, Jackson.

12. Rivers Cottrell Wall to Nannie Dunlap Finley, 31 Jan 1905, AM/SPF; undated obituary of Nannie Dunlap Finley, AM/SPF; George T. Finley estate papers, AM/SPF; George T. Finley obituary, Holly Springs *South Reporter*, 2 Aug 1921; telephone interviews by author with L. A. Smith III, 13 Mar 2006, and Willie Hayes Mallory, 15 Mar 2006.

Chapter 13. *Sharecropping in the Depression*

1. Returns for Inheritance Taxes on Estate of George T. Finley and List of Finley Rents 1921, both in AM/SPF.

2. Roger L. Ransom and Richard Sutch, *One Kind of Freedom: The Economic Consequences of Emancipation*, 2nd ed. (Cambridge: Cambridge University Press, 2001), xi–xvi; Giles, "Agricultural Revolution, 1890–1970," 181; James Elihue Howell interview, 13 Nov 2003, SPOHP; transcription of Feb 2006 interview with Mamie Dowdy by Willie H. Mallory, McAlexander Collection.

3. Interview of Martha V. Moseley by author, 28 Dec 1980; Giles, "Agricultural Revolution, 1890–1970," 197; Marshall County Deed Book 73, 430, Book 76, 457–458, Book 77, 153.

4. Giles, "Agricultural Revolution, 1890–1970," 190, 197.

5. Obituaries in Holly Springs *South Reporter* of John P. Davis, 1 Dec 1927, and Eben N. Davis, 18 Jul 1935; 1930 census of Marshall County, Beat 1, 9B, family no. 165; Mrs. E. J. Taylor to E. L. McAlexander, 29 Oct 1920, and 17 Jan 1926, both in McAlexander Collection; interview with Nell Fitts Beswick by author, 15 Jun 2005.

6. Giles, "Agricultural Revolution, 1890–1970," 197; Ruthie Shelton interview, 11 Nov 2004, SPOHP; 1933 Thomas Finley farm ledger, AM/SPF.

7. Ruthie Shelton interview, 11 Nov 2004, SPOHP; Mallory, "When I Can Read My Title Clear," 93.

8. Idalia Harris Holloway interview, 6 Nov 2003, SPOHP.

9. 1870 Marshall County census, 30, family no. 268; Idalia Harris Holloway interview, 6 Nov 2003, SPOHP; Fannie Oliver Zinn interview, 27 Sept 2004, SPOHP.

10. Grace Mallory Turner interviews, 28 Jan 2004 and 26 Mar 2004, SPOHP.

11. Idalia Harris Holloway interview, 6 Nov 2003; Fannie Oliver Zinn interview, 24 Feb 2004; Fannie Jones Martin interview, 24 Feb 2004, all SPOHP.

12. Holloway interview, 6 Nov 2003; Zinn interview, 24 Feb 2004, both SPOHP.

13. Mallory, "When I Can Read My Title Clear," 76, 90.

14. James Howell interview, 13 Nov 2003, SPOHP; Mallory, "When I Can Read My Title Clear," 70, 90, 77, 83, 96.

15. Interview with Mamie Dowdy by Willie H. Mallory, Feb 2006, transcript in McAlexander Collection; Marshall County Deed Book 159, 309.

16. Ransom and Sutch, *One Kind of Freedom*, 195; Mallory, "When I Can Read My Title Clear," 38.

Chapter 14. *A Family's Values*

1. Undated Leach clippings in AM/SPF; obituary of J. G. Leach, Holly Springs *South*, 28 April 1904; Butt-Leach information, interview with Nancy Fant Smith by author, 10 Sept 2004; Winter (ed.), *Amid Some Excellent Company*, 26, 28.

2. Leach family information from Nancy Fant Smith, 10 Sept 2004.

3. J. G. Leach obituary, Holly Springs *South*, 28 April 1904.

4. Telephone interview with Nancy Fant Smith by author, 2 Feb 2006; Giles, "Agricultural Revolution, 1890–1970," 194, 203; Marshall County Deed Book 77, 97; Janice Tyler Calame interview, 18 Sept 2003, SPOHP.

5. Interview with Nancy Fant Smith by author, 10 Sept 2004.

6. Janice Tyler Calame interview, 18 Sept 2003, Chesley Thorne Smith interview, 7 Aug 2003, both SPOHP.

7. Chesley Thorne Smith interview, 7 Aug 2003, SPOHP; Janice Tyler Calame interview, 18 Sept 2003, SPOHP; Registrar, University of Mississippi to Ruth Finley, 29 Oct 1931, AM/SPF; interview with Nancy Fant Smith by author, 30 Jun 2003.

8. Interview with Nancy Fant Smith by author, 2 Feb 2006; Janice Tyler Calame interview, 18 Sept 2003, SPOHP; undated clippings on the Finley-Shackelford engagement from the Memphis *Commercial Appeal* and the Oklahoma City *Daily Oklahoman*, AM/SPF; Margaret Finley Shackelford curriculum vitae, SPAC; Frances Buchanan, Nyla Moore, and Dorothy Warren interview, 11 Aug 2003, SPOHP.

9. Buchanan, Moore, and Warren interview, 11 Aug 2003, and Roxie Holloway interview, 20 Jul 2004, SPOHP.

10. *Daily Oklahoman*, 6 Aug 1961, and Ruth Leach Finley to Margaret Finley Shackelford, 10 Mar 1966, both in AM/SPF.

11. Telephone interviews by author with Nancy Fant Smith, 2 Feb 2006, L. A. Smith III, 10 Jan 2007, and Lester G. Fant III, 8 Jan 2007.

12. Thomas M. Bell and Fred E. M. Gillham, *The World of Cotton* (Washington, D.C.: ContiCotton, EMR, 2001), 3; Giles, "Agricultural Revolution, 1890–1970," 203–204, 209; James N. Gregory, *The Southern Diaspora* (Chapel Hill: University of North Carolina Press, 2005), 24, 34; McAlexander, *A Southern Tapestry*, 134.

13. Interview by author with L. A. Smith III, 13 Mar 2006.

14. James "Boe" McClure interview, 28 Jan 2004, SPOHP; R. A. McPherson to Ruth Finley, 24 Dec 1971, SPAC.

15. Margaret Finley Shackelford to Thomas L. Kimball, National Wildlife Foundation, 4 Dec 1968, SPAC.

16. Boe and Melton McClure interview, 23 Oct 2003, SPOHP; recommendation of W. Carlyle Blakeney Jr. to National Audubon Society Board of Directors, copy attached to Blakeney letter to Ruth Finley and Dr. and Mrs. John Shackelford, 29 Nov 1982, SPAC.

17. Martha Virginia Moseley (30 Oct 1894–11 Jan 1986) had wished to be buried in the family cemetery at Strawberry Plains, but Margaret Finley Shackelford, worried about danger to the cemetery from the erosion of the high bluff by the branch of the Coldwater River, thought it best that she be buried in Hill Crest Cemetery in Holly Springs. She was interred in one of the lots of the Brittenum family.

18. Hugh H. Rather, architect's drawing, AM/SPF; Clarence Coleman, as quoted by Bobby Mitchell to author, 15 Mar 2006.

19. Photograph of Peggy Smith Kallaher on the staircase at her wedding reception at Shrine Club, Memphis, 3 May 1952, SPAC; telephone interview with Madge Lindsay by author, 8 Nov 2006.

20. Charles N. Dean to author, 4 Nov 1974, McAlexander Collection.

21. Among the historically significant objects gathered at Strawberry Plains is a beaded workbox inherited from "Nanna," Anna Parham Leach. Made by her aunts Martha Ann Elizabeth Parham and Mary Jane Gilliam Parham (b. 1813) during their school days in southside Virginia, it is a fine example of folk art, which Ruth Finley had once considered giving to Winterthur.

22. Robert E. Tyson, M.D., to Ruth Finley, 21 Aug 1979, AM/SPF; Marie S. Moore, "Audubon Society Given Finley Land, Antebellum Homes," *Pigeon Roost News*, 19 Jan 1983.

23. Glenn Olson, National Audubon Society, to Mrs. John Shackelford, 1 Jun 1996 and 10 May 1997; Donal C. O'Brien Jr., National Audubon Society, to Mrs. John Shackelford, 10 Mar 1998, all at SPAC.

24. The Rev. Dr. R. Milton Winter, Meditation for the Funeral of Margaret Finley Shackelford, 10 Oct 1998, McAlexander Collection.

Chapter 15. Audubon Center

1. Holly Wright, "State Audubon Society Creating a 'Culture of Conservation' among Mississippians through Educational Programs," Holly Springs *South Reporter*, 25 Feb 1999, sec. 3, 7; "Audubon Sanctuary to Cultivate Land Ethic," *Mississippi Audubon* (Winter 2001), 6.

2. Ruth A. Finley, Margaret Finley Shackelford, and Robert Crutcher to National Audubon Society, [statement on "proposed nature and conservation preserve"], 20 Oct 1982, SPAC; Jesse Grantham, "A Gift to Mississippi," *Mississippi Audubon* (Winter 2001), 2.

3. *Mississippi Audubon* (Winter 2001), 6, 2, 3; "Strawberry Plains Audubon Center: A Plan for the Future, Winter 2001," submitted to Shackelford Trust, courtesy of Paul Calame, 35–36.

4. "A Plan for the Future," 3, 30, 7.

5. "A Plan for the Future," 7–8, 12, 42, 36, 20, 25, 23, 30, 4. See Stephen J. Pyne, *Fire in America: A Cultural History of Wildland and Rural Fire* (Princeton, N.J.: Princeton University Press, 1982).

6. Steve Brewer and Sherry Bell-Surrette, Preliminary Report, 20 Jan 2003, and Final Report: Ecological Restoration of Natural Fire Regimes in Oak-Hickory Communities at the Strawberry Plains Audubon Center, 19 Sept 2003, both at SPAC.

7. "Strawberry Plains Assembles History Steering Committee," *South Reporter*, 13 Jul 2003, sec. 2, 7; History Steering Committee Minutes, 24 Jun 2003, SPAC.

8. Sue Watson, "The Humming Birds Are Coming Soon," *South Reporter*, 28 Aug 2003, sec. 2, 1; Report for Shackelford Trust Advisors Meeting, 31 Jul 2003, courtesy of Paul Calame.

9. Terrance R. Weik, Ph.D., Preliminary Archeological Survey of the Strawberry Plains Audubon Center, 22 April 2003, and Robert C. Watson, report on Vernacular Architecture, African-American History, 10 April 2003, both at SPAC; "Strawberry Plains Prepares for Archeological Dig," *South Reporter*, 11 Dec 2003, sec. 2, 5; Jay K. Johnson and Bryan S. Haley, Geophysical Survey of Historic Sites

Located at Strawberry Plains Audubon Center, Holly Springs, Mississippi, 20 Jun 2004, SPAC; Terrance Weik, Phase 1 Archeological Survey of the Strawberry Plains Audubon Center, Dec 2004, SPAC.

10. Louidean Ball, "Forestry Field Day at Strawberry Plains," *South Reporter*, 30 Oct 2003, sec. 2, 5; Second History Steering Committee Meeting Minutes, 18 Dec 2003, SPAC; Sue Watson, "Audubon Reviews Progress," *South Reporter*, 15 Jan 2004, 1; "Strawberry Plains Audubon Center Embarks on Strategic Planning Process," *South Reporter*, 16 Jun 2004, sec. 2, 3; Sue Watson, "Audubon Oral History Project Records Community Stories," *South Reporter*, 15 Jul 2004, 1, 15; "Audubon Center to Present Program Saturday on Archaeological Studies," *South Reporter*, 14 Oct 2004, 15; Sue Watson, "Audubon Program Summarizes Results of Historical Studies," *South Reporter*, 21 Oct 2004, sec. 1, 16.

11. Sue Watson, "Audubon Launches Education Initiative," *South Reporter*, 11 Mar 2004, sec 4, 5; "Strawberry Plains Audubon Center Announces Education Programs," *South Reporter*, 10 Jan 2004, 4; "Strawberry Plains Hosts Student Scientific Exhibit," *South Reporter*, 28 Feb 2004, 13; "Strawberry Plains Hosts Student Naturalist Camp," *South Reporter*, 5 Jun 2004, 3; Sue Watson, "Audubon Answers Kids' Questions," *South Reporter*, 11 Nov 2004, 16.

12. Sue Watson, "First Lady Tours Strawberry Plains," *South Reporter*, 5 Jul 2004, 1; "Thousands Turn out for Hummingbirds," *South Reporter*, 20 Sept 2004, 1, 4; "Humming Celebration September 9–11," *South Reporter*, 30 Aug 2005, 3.

13. Report for Shackelford Trust Advisors Meeting, 11 Nov 2004, courtesy of Paul Calame; Alan Huffman, "Strawberry Plains Forever," *Preservation* 57 (Mar/April 2005), 32–36.

14. Barry Burleson, "Plantation Office Saved, Moved to Strawberry Plains," *South Reporter*, 9 Jun 2005, 1, 13; "Saving a Piece of History," *South Reporter*, 25 Aug 2005, 1; letter to donors from Chelius H. Carter, 15 Aug 2005, McAlexander Collection.

15. "Hummingbird Celebration September 9–11," *South Reporter*, 30 Aug 2005, 3; "Celebrating Audubon's 100th in Style," *Audubon Mississippi* [note name change] (Fall/Winter 2005), 6.

16. Report for Shackelford Trust Advisors Meeting, FY 05 and 31 Jul 2006; "The Coldwater River," *Audubon Mississippi* (Fall/Winter 2006), 6.

17. Quoted in Huffman, "Strawberry Plains Forever," 36.

INDEX